Othello

ARDEN STUDENT SKILLS: LANGUAGE AND WRITING

Series Editor:

Dympna Callaghan, Syracuse University

Published Titles

The Tempest, Brinda Charry
Macbeth, Emma Smith
Romeo and Juliet, Catherine Belsey

Forthcoming Titles

Hamlet, Dympna Callaghan
Twelfth Night, Frances E. Dolan
King Lear, Jean Howard
A Midsummer Night's Dream, Heidi Brayman Hackel

Othello

Language and Writing

LAURIE MAGUIRE

B L O O M S B U R Y
LONDON • NEW DELHI • NEW YORK • SYDNEY

Bloomsbury Arden Shakespeare

An imprint of Bloomsbury Publishing Plc

50 Bedford Square	1385 Broadway
London	New York
WC1B 3DP	NY 10018
UK	USA

www.bloomsbury.com

Bloomsbury is a registered trade mark of Bloomsbury Publishing Plc

British Library Cataloguing-in-Publication Data

A catalogue record for this book is available from the British Library.

ISBN: HB: 978-1-4725-1829-3
PB: 978-1-4081-5659-9
ePDF: 978-1-4725-1830-9
ePub: 978-1-4081-7067-0

Library of Congress Cataloging-in-Publication Data

A catalog record for this book is available from the Library of Congress

Typeset by Fakenham Prepress Solutions, Fakenham, Norfolk NR21 8NN
Printed and bound in Great Britain

CONTENTS

ACKNOWLEDGEMENTS

My explorations of language in *Othello* have been accompanied and enabled by the knowledge and interrogative labours of Aleksandra Thostrup. No mere research assistant, she has been a happy collaborator: her fingerprints are perhaps most noticeable in Chapter 3 but her influence is everywhere. I am particularly indebted to her for material on coney-catching pamphlets, on bawdy courts, on modals, puns and metaphors, and for contributions to the 'Writing matters' sections. At a late stage Samuel Plumb road-tested this linguistic ride for accessibility and offered helpful suggestions about film. Sophie Duncan typed up my manuscript musings. I am hugely grateful to all three.

SERIES EDITOR'S PREFACE

This series puts the pedagogical expertise of distinguished literary critics at the disposal of students embarking upon Shakespeare Studies at university. While they demonstrate a variety of approaches to the plays, all the contributors to the series share a deep commitment to teaching and a wealth of knowledge about the culture and history of Shakespeare's England. The approach of each of the volumes is direct yet intellectually sophisticated and tackles the challenges Shakespeare presents. These volumes do not provide a short-cut to Shakespeare's works but instead offer a careful explication of them directed towards students' own processing and interpretation of the plays and poems.

Students' needs in relation to Shakespeare revolve overwhelmingly around language, and Shakespeare's language is what most distinguishes him from his rivals and collaborators – as well as what most embeds him in his own historical moment. The *Language and Writing* series understands language as the very heart of Shakespeare's literary achievement rather than as an obstacle to be circumvented. This series addresses the difficulties often encountered in reading Shakespeare alongside the necessity of writing papers for university examinations and course assessment. The primary objective here is to foster rigorous critical engagement with the texts by helping students develop their own critical writing skills. *Language and Writing* titles demonstrate how to develop students' own capacity to articulate and enlarge upon their experience of encountering the text, far beyond summarizing, paraphrasing or 'translating' Shakespeare's language into a more palatable, contemporary form. Each of the volumes in the series introduces the text as an act of specifically literary language and shows that the multifarious issues of life and history that Shakespeare's work addresses cannot be separated from their expression in language. In addition, each book takes students through a series of guidelines about how to develop viable undergraduate critical essays on the text in question, not by delivering interpretations, but rather by taking readers step-by-step through the process of discovering and developing their own critical ideas.

All the books include chapters examining the text from the point of view of its composition, that is, from the perspective of Shakespeare's own process of composition as a reader, thinker and writer. The opening chapters consider when and how the play was written, addressing, for example, the extant literary and cultural acts of language, from which Shakespeare constructed his work – including his sources – as well as the generic, literary and theatrical conventions at his disposal. Subsequent sections demonstrate how to engage in detailed examination and analysis of the text and focus on the literary, technical and historical intricacies of Shakespeare's verse and prose. Each volume also includes some discussion of performance. Other chapters cover textual issues as well as the interpretation of the extant texts for any given play on stage and screen, treating for example, the use of stage directions or parts of the play that are typically cut in performance. Authors also address issues of stage/film history as they relate to the cultural evolution of Shakespeare's words. In addition, these chapters deal with the critical reception of the work, particularly the newer theoretical and historicist approaches that have revolutionized our understanding of Shakespeare's language over the past 40 years. Crucially, every chapter contains a section on 'Writing matters', which links the analysis of Shakespeare's language with students' own critical writing.

The series empowers students to read and write about Shakespeare with scholarly confidence and hopes to inspire their enthusiasm for doing so. The authors in this series have been selected because they combine scholarly distinction with outstanding teaching skills. Each book exposes the reader to an eminent scholar's teaching in action and expresses a vocational commitment to making Shakespeare accessible to a new generation of student readers.

Professor Dympna Callaghan
Series Editor
Arden Student Skills: Language and Writing

PREFACE

Othello is a play about uncoupling.

At one level, this seems obvious: the plot shows Iago's success in severing the newly married Othello and Desdemona. But at the linguistic level, Iago also severs bonds: the union between word and meaning. Thus, uncoupling is both his goal and his strategy; he breaks the ties of a human marital union by breaking ties in a semantic union – the relationship between a word (a 'signifier') and the image or meaning (the 'signified') that is conveyed or signified by that word. The play reverses and inverts associations and meanings so that Desdemona's 'virtue' appears 'pitch' (2.3.355) and Othello's most perfidious associate appears his most 'honest' friend.

Iago's subtle manipulation of words not only creates a profoundly unstable linguistic world for the play's unsuspecting hero: it opens the door to misinterpretation. Iago puts a wedge between words and facts, between language and reality, then hands the power of interpretation to Othello: 'what you will' he tells him when Othello, in a conversation about proof of Desdemona's infidelity, asks for clarification of Iago's hints. Iago has just said that Cassio, Desdemona's alleged lover, has 'said that he did – I know not what he did'. This evasion naturally prompts Othello to ask 'What? What?'. Iago replies, still evasively but more allusively, with a free-floating verb: 'Lie'. The clarification that Othello now requests is not just sexual but grammatical: he wants to know the relation between subject and object, and so he supplies a preposition and an object: 'With her?'. Iago answers: 'With her, on her, *what you will*' (4.1.34, my italics). As Emma Smith shows, in another book in this series, *Macbeth*, Macbeth's 'misinterpretation of the witches' prophecy is fatal' (Smith 2013, xliii). Iago is to Othello what the witches are to Macbeth: a speaker whose ambiguity prompts the hero to tragic and fatal misinterpretation.

All literary interpretation is based on analysis of language; that is the foundational skill taught and perfected in English literature courses from school to university. It is also a skill we require in daily life whether in business, politics or family situations. On a daily basis we assess what people say, what they want, what they say they want, what they don't want. We pay as much attention to their silences as to their utterances. We constantly evaluate textual evidence ('that's patronizing', we think; or 'that's rather generous'); their euphemisms (are they uncomfortable? Are they concealing something?); their logic or illogic ('there's something missing here'); their timing ('why did they raise this subject now?'); their deviations from their normal attitude or expressions ('has something changed?'). As a play in which the hero misinterprets language, and in which the villain deliberately engineers situations that make this misunderstanding possible, *Othello* is of particular interest and relevance to us – not just as students of English but as human beings who engage in the making and interpretation of meaning in all aspects of our linguistic life. Iago works via every item in my list above – euphemism, silence, evasion, illogic, timing – and Othello changes his beliefs and expressions. Analysing these linguistic strategies and their tragic effects will help us understand how transactional meaning is created both in literary works like *Othello* and in our own prose compositions (as well as in the linguistic environment that we, as humans, inhabit).

When Iago muses on the potential reversals that his plot(s) will engineer, he tells Roderigo 'The food that to him [Othello] now is as luscious as locusts [carob juice] shall be to him shortly as acerb as coloquintida [bitter as the colocynth fruit – a sour apple]' (1.3.348–50). We see here Iago's awareness (conscious or subliminal?) that the destruction he effects is linguistic: he will not only change Othello's emotions and relationship but will change the terms of similes: 'as luscious as locusts' becomes 'as acerb as coloquintida'. Iago alters language, metaphor, correspondence. And he presents this statement to Roderigo in a way that grammatically occludes his own role in the destruction of the marriage: 'food' is the subject of the sentence, not Iago; it is the food that changes its taste not Iago who changes Othello's perception ('The food … shall be …', not 'I shall make the food seem …'). Iago initiates the play's tragedy but his language consistently suppresses his agency. When he describes Cassio as a 'slipper and subtle knave' (2.1.239–40), we cannot help but reflect that this is a more accurate description of Iago himself. Consequently, we, as readers, must be more than usually vigilant in paying attention to his 'slipper and subtle' linguistic tactics.

This book

In a book about language it is difficult to keep categories separate. Selecting one item for scrutiny – a word, an image, narrative, interpretation, meaning, ambiguity – brings all the other items with it, just as pulling out one spaghetti strand brings a forkful. I have divided this book into three main topics – chapters on narrative, genre and boundaries – but since language is intrinsic to them all, there is a degree of overlap. I hope that when later chapters revisit material from earlier chapters, placing it in a different context, it functions as a helpful refrain rather than a redundant repetition.

Chapter 1, 'Language and narrative', examines the play's interest in story-telling. *Othello* begins and ends in story-telling: Othello not only woos and wins Desdemona with tales of adventure but is asked to recount this wooing in a narrative of self-justification to the Senate in Act One; the play ends with Othello offering a brief autobiography before he commits suicide. In between, the play is very interested in the power of story-telling and the difficulties of interpretation. I begin with this chapter on larger narrative issues as they enable us to look at the big picture – the relation between speakers and hearers, for instance, or the play's structure in which multiple or contradictory versions of stories are offered – before we analyse linguistic details in the way the play's stories are manipulated or constructed (Iago's use of euphemism, for example). The chapter concludes by returning to the issue of narrative with which it began, interrogating Othello's final request that we speak of him 'as I am' – a request that, given the difficulties of narrative the chapter has explored, is not as straightforward as it seems.

Chapter 2, 'Language and genre', picks up a staple of *Othello* criticism – that the play begins as comedy and ends as tragedy. It may seem odd to devote an entire chapter to genre in a book about language but the key question of this chapter is whether genre has linguistic as well as structural markers. How do we know when we are in the world of comedy or of tragedy? Does comedy do different things with its language from tragedy? Is there a linguistic overlap between the two genres or are they totally separate? In thinking about the language of *Othello* and its tragic effect, I end with versions of *Othello* that lack Shakespeare's language: a 1620s adaptation by the playwright John Ford and two film adaptations from the twenty-first century. I find the film adaptations more tragically powerful than the Ford play and try to work out why this might be.

Chapter 3, 'Language and boundaries', picks up linguistic issues from the previous two chapters and looks at them in more detail. Some of the issues are technical – how Iago exploits the verb 'to be' or how the play uses puns. Others are thematic – how the play's interest in boundaries relates to topics such as identity (the difference between self and other), to theatre (the relationship between performer and audience) and what happens when language crosses boundaries (as when Othello starts to speak with Iago's vocabulary). This, I think, is the most challenging chapter (for the author in writing as for the reader in reception). This is partly because of the way the chapter analyses as discrete units things that are not easily kept separate (language, character, power: look at the five sections that are about puns – only three of which have 'pun' or 'puns' in their heading); and it is partly because much of what this chapter analyses could equally belong in earlier chapters. That, of course, is one of the interesting points about language as a topic: *everything* is to do with language at some level. Since this is a book about writing, you might like to look at the frequency with which this chapter cross-references earlier chapters (or the way earlier chapters promise later development in this one) and work out why the material I have chosen to discuss here is included in this chapter. I have classified all this chapter's topics under the general heading of 'boundaries' but my preliminary thinking had a number of alternative general headings which would tie this material together differently. (Maybe you can supply some alternatives that you would prefer.) And while we are thinking about writing (or while you are thinking about your own writing, now or later), it might help you to know that I originally envisaged this chapter as being the first in the book (and I wrote it first). It seemed to me a good idea to start with some really nitty-gritty issue of language, particularly Iago's language, and then move outwards from there (for example, how the problems in his use of the verb 'to be' affect questions of identity in the play). After I had finished the book I decided that this material was problematic at the book's threshold and so relocated it to the end (and revised it accordingly). Can you work out what my reasons were in feeling/doing this? Would you have preferred this chapter as the first?

Chapter 4, 'Writing tips and topics', begins with general advice for writing argumentative prose and then moves to four topics that might provide fruitful work for further research and writing. In offering suggestions about how one might go about interrogating these topics, I indicate a variety of different approaches and questions. There is no blueprint for academic thought or writing; part of the intellectual excitement of research comes from discovering the different perspectives one can have on the same topic if one sets up the opening question(s) differently. 'Race', for instance, meant something different in 1600 from what it means in the twenty-first century. And between Shakespeare's day and ours are 400 years of cultural politics (and political atrocity) with performance histories of *Othello* that give the play different 'meanings' at different moments (in separationist USA, or apartheid South Africa, for instance). This chapter stresses, therefore, the importance of recognizing a critic's entry point and knowing one's own critical perspective when formulating an argument. One does not need to use critical labels – it is enough just to be aware that someone like Thomas Rymer (whose seventeenth-century response to *Othello* we will examine in Chapter 2), was writing at a period that valued 'decorum' and elegance, so the mixture of comedy and tragedy in *Othello* that appeals to us today (and may have seemed ambitiously experimental in Shakespeare's day) was obviously going to antagonize him.

As we shall see in the main chapters in this book, the language of *Othello* draws on legal rhetoric and legal terminology, on classical rhetoric with its formal rules of structure and technique, on vocabulary and images in plays by Shakespeare's predecessors and contemporaries, on addresses to the audience by the Vice in medieval drama, on the linguistic trickery of a stranger by a local resident in pamphlets of the 1590s, on slanderous sexual insults made about women by women and brought to trial in church courts ... It is not necessary to be aware of all these different linguistic registers. But in writing about any one of them in the play, it is important to be aware of the *kind* of language it represents and why: legal vocabulary is relevant in a play about justice, for instance. And it can alert us to issues beyond language: the play has a judicial-scene structure, from Othello's opening defence in the Senate to his final scene where the bedroom becomes a court in which Desdemona is sentenced. Analysing the different linguistic currents that flow into *Othello* is the purpose of this book.

Before Chapters 1 to 3 grapple with linguistic detail, the Introduction provides an overview of a variety of key topics that will help situate the play for you. It looks at the story of the Moor and Desdemona that Shakespeare found in an Italian novella, at the emotional and rhetorical impact on audiences of the first actor to play Othello, at the play's locations, its women, its props, and at the two texts of *Othello* (Shakespeare seems to have revised the play, making major and minor changes). These general topics will feed into all the later chapters. The book works in an aggregative fashion, building up topics, cross-referencing them, returning to rethink earlier topics in the light of new discussions. But each chapter also works, and can be read, independently.

Introduction

Narrating *Othello*

The story of *Othello* first appeared in an Italian work, a collection of tales by the Renaissance poet Giovanni Battista Giraldi Cinthio, *Gli Hecatommithi* (1565). Like the medieval *Decameron* by Giovanni Boccaccio (written 1350–3), in which ten people tell ten tales each, and the contemporary *Novelle* (*Tales*) by Matteo Bandello (1554), Cinthio's collection is narrated by a variety of story-tellers. The stories are thematically linked: each tale debates or illustrates an aspect of love and marriage, from choosing a mate to being unfaithful. In English, Cinthio's title means *One Hundred Stories* (Boccaccio's title translates as *Ten-Day Event* and, with its ten stories and narrators, also totals one hundred tales). Cinthio's story is very short and can be accessed easily (it is reprinted at the end of E. A. J. Honigmann's edition of *Othello* – this is the translation from which I quote – as well as in Michael Neill's edition of the play).

In outline, Cinthio's story is the same as Shakespeare's: Disdemona (Cinthio's spelling), 'a virtuous Lady of wondrous beauty' (Honigmann, 371) marries a Moor against the wishes of her family. Venice sends the Moor to Cyprus for military reasons. An ensign 'of handsome presence but the most scoundrelly nature in the world' (373) falls in love with Disdemona. She has eyes only for her husband so the ensign's love turns to hate; he concludes that her indifference to him must be because she is attracted to a corporal 'who was very dear to the Moor' (373). The ensign determines to kill both Disdemona and the corporal.

Cinthio is a more talented writer than my blunt summary makes him sound. He is not a novelist, as we understand the term, but his story bowls along. It has a broader sweep than Shakespeare's. After Disdemona's death, the Moor realizes that the ensign is to blame and he ostracizes him. The ensign continues to injure the Moor, this time via the corporal, to whom he reveals the Moor's role in Disdemona's murder. Back in Venice, the corporal accuses the Moor. The Moor denies everything, is nonetheless imprisoned then exiled, and then, we are told, almost in an afterthought and certainly not a detailed one, 'he was finally slain by Disdemona's relatives as he richly deserved' (385).

The ensign continues in his scoundrelly ways until a new offence leads him to trial and torture, where he 'was tortured so fiercely that his inner organs were ruptured' (386). The tale concludes with some moral underlining by Cinthio: 'thus did God avenge the innocence of Disdemona'. The auditors of the tale 'praised God because the criminals had had suitable punishment' (386). Things are thus tied up morally but there is no dramatic public showdown. The ensign's wife survives, unlike Shakespeare's Emilia, and because she has been privy to her husband's machinations (again unlike Emilia), reveals all the events, after his death. How, to whom, in what circumstances, we do not know. Cinthio is interested in the morals to be drawn: the foolishness of the over-credulous Moor, the malignity of the human heart.

If Cinthio's story is extended in time scheme and anticlimactic in denouement (*denouement* is the French term adopted by English for the final unravelling of events), it is more dramatic in other – non-stageable – ways. Disdemona's death is engineered to look like an accident. The ensign bludgeons her to death with a stocking full of sand, then he and the Moor cause the ceiling to fall in. A strategically placed rafter by Disdemona's head makes her look like the victim of architectural accident. Shakespeare's choice of strangling is more manageable. It is also more thematically relevant in a play about language; and in a play that repeatedly silences women

(Emilia, Bianca, Desdemona), Shakespeare's Desdemona loses her voice, her breath, her life.

Cinthio's ensign has a three-year-old daughter who is instrumental in enabling the ensign to steal the handkerchief (which is a deliberately planned act rather than an accidental opportunity – the ensign's thoughts 'twist ... and turn ... in all directions' until he thinks up the handkerchief theft as a 'new piece of mischief'; 377). Very small children are not impossible on the Elizabethan stage (Mamillius in *The Winter's Tale* may be as young as five) but they are rare, for obvious reasons, so Shakespeare removes this domestic detail. One of the things that is remarkable about *Othello* is how much we know about Othello (his royal descent, his military background, the length of time he has spent in Venetian civilian life, how he met Desdemona) and how little we know about Iago. (See Honigmann's note at 3.4.138: 'In this scene we hear of Othello's father, mother, brother, of the Egyptian, the sibyl – i.e. his background'.) Apart from one unusually precise detail – Iago's age (28: 'I have looked upon the world for four times seven year'; 1.3.312–13) – we are given no background information about Iago, and Cinthio's domestic details are removed.

Although the removal of the three-year-old daughter is primarily practical in origin, it is also part of a series of changes Shakespeare makes which enhance the role of chance and coincidence. Cinthio's ensign steals the handkerchief; Shakespeare's simply receives it. Cinthio tells us that the ensign 'had great sleight of hand' and, under cover of transferring the child from his arms to Disdemona's, he carefully takes the handkerchief 'from her girdle so warily that she did not notice it' (378). Throughout the play Shakespeare's Iago is more an opportunist than a strategist. We see him regularly in the process of working things out on the spot – 'let me see now' (1.3.391) – or admitting that he has not quite worked things out yet – ''Tis here, but yet confused' (2.1.309). Even as he stages the Cyprus brawl he is talking in vague terms: 'now ... / Am I to put our Cassio in some action / That may offend the isle' (2.3.56–8). 'Some' action – the plan is still not quite clear.

Elsewhere in the play, Iago's soliloquies only give the illusion of clarity: he tells us what he is doing but not why he is doing it. In soliloquy he presents himself as someone revealing confidences to us, as 'honest Iago'. But his dealings with us are only a variant of his dealings with Othello: he manipulates Othello with ambiguous language and he manipulates us with fake clarity.

Name and identity

The only character given a name in Cinthio's story is Disdemona. Shakespeare adds a name for the Moor – Othello; for the ensign – Iago; for the corporal (whom he elevates to lieutenant) – Michael Cassio; and for Cassio's girlfriend/ prostitute – Bianca. In a play which examines the relationship between word and meaning (as we noted, briefly, in the Preface and as we shall see at greater length in Chapters One to Three), Shakespeare offers the relationship between name and identity as a subset exploration of the larger category of word/meaning. Early modern discussions of language often slide in their examples between proper names and common nouns. This slippage is endemic to language because proper names belong to a taxonomy of referring expressions (*taxonomy* is the branch of science to do with classification); the questions raised by the dyad of name/identity are also posed by word/thing. The ancient Greek philosopher Plato acknowlededges that not all words are names but names are words (Fine 292, 290). For Plato's student, Aristotle, a name was a word which belongs to someone or something (Harris and Taylor, 20). For the early Christian theologian, Saint Augustine, 'All things that are words are also names' (Augustine, 121).

Cassio's professional demotion is linked to loss of personal name: Othello moves from the closeness of the given name

('How comes it, *Michael*, you are thus forgot?') to the distance of the surname ('*Cassio*, I love thee, / But never more be officer of mine'; 2.3.184, 244–5, my emphases). One critic argues that Iago's revenge tactic is to annihilate both personal name and positional name (father, husband, wife, lieutenant, general, governor): 'Brabantio declares in anguish he no longer has a daughter, Cassio that he has lost his name and rank, Desdemona that she has lost her lord, and Othello that his occupation is gone, that he has no wife, and finally that he is no longer "Othello"' (Watson, 339–40).

At the end of the tale in Cinthio, some of the auditors blame Disdemona's father for giving her such an inauspicious name – it means 'unfortunate' in Greek. We might also blame Shakespeare for giving the unnamed ensign of the source the name Iago (the name of Spain's patron saint, famous for conquering the Moors). In 939 CE Santiago (Saint Iago or Saint James) helped King Ramirez deliver Castile from the Moors, killing 60,000 Moors in battle. Consequently 'Santiago' became the war-cry of the Spanish armies and Santiago is traditionally depicted on a white charger trampling the Moors underfoot. Iago's role, as destroyer of Othello, the Moor of Venice, is thus cued by his name; word matches thing, his behaviour supports the sign.

The handkerchief

Cinthio's corporal has a domestic woman in his house who does sewing and embroidery for him. It is she who is instructed to copy the design on Disdemona's handkerchief before the corporal returns it to her. Elizabethan handkerchiefs were large items so we must rid ourselves of the notion of the small 10-inch square. In the play, Desdemona has a logical reason to believe that she can bind Othello's head with her hankie, although he protests that it is too little. (His protest is as much metaphorical as practical: no handkerchief can be large enough to bind up the pain of his being cuckolded.) In an anonymous play, probably by Thomas Heywood, called *The Fair Maid of the Exchange* (printed in 1607), a linen embroiderer is instructed to stitch decorations in the four corners of a handkerchief. In one corner is to be 'wanton Love, / Drawing his bow, shooting an amorous dart'; in the opposite corner is 'an arrow in a heart'; a third corner has the allegorical figure of Disdain; in the fourth is 'a springing laurel-tree, / Circled about with a ring of poesy [poetry]' (Act 2, scene 2, pp. 33–4). The 'ring of poesy' comprises no fewer than four lines – lines which, as it happens, explain the decorations in all the corners (Act 2, scene 2, p. 34). If this is not parodic (and there may be an element of comedy in the lengthy lines of poetry), it is a huge amount of detail and space. It tells us a lot about the size of Desdemona's handkerchief – it is a highly visible stage prop.

Cinthio tells us simply that the handkerchief was embroidered in Moorish fashion (378). Shakespeare himself embroiders this vagueness into the specificity of the strawberry motif. The strawberry is associated with virginity and the Virgin Mary (because it is an innocent fruit – Satan tempted Eve with a fruit that grows on a tree). An influential article in the 1970s (by Lynda Boose) argued that this red motif on the handkerchief's white background reproduces in miniature the nuptial sheets stained with blood as proof of virginity. Mosaic law decreed that the bride's family should display the ocular 'proof of the bride's virginity' (i.e. bloodstained sheets) in public; inability to do so resulted in the bride being stoned to death (Deuteronomy 21.13–21). The custom was still recognizable in early modern England. Henry VIII's first wife, Catherine of Aragon, kept her wedding sheets for over 30 years, producing them as evidence in the divorce case brought by Henry against her. Thus, it is because the handkerchief emblematizes Desdemona's virginity that her failure to produce it results in her death.

One critic has recently questioned this narrative by interrogating the colour of the handkerchief. Ian Smith's research suggests that Desdemona's handkerchief is black, not white as conventionally assumed. (The critical assumption that it should be white is itself matter for investigation in this play's Eurocentric history of racial assumptions.) The handkerchief is described as being dyed. Specifically, it is 'dyed in mummy' (3.4.76), a black liquid believed to come from mummified corpses (in keeping with the handkerchief's Egyptian provenance: 'that handkerchief / Did an Egyptian to my mother give'; 3.4.57–8). The strange detail offered by Emilia – that Desdemona 'so loves the token ... / That she reserves it evermore about her / To kiss and talk to' (3.3.297, 299–300) – makes sense if the love token is a black textile representing her husband (women do not otherwise kiss and talk to hankies). When Desdemona talks about Othello in Act Four (she says 'I know not how I lost him'; 4.2.153), her language reminds us of her similar perplexity over the loss of the handkerchief: 'where should I lose that handkerchief?' (3.4.23; cf. her repetition at 3.4.102–3). 'Closely identified with Othello, the handkerchief is a substitute self' (Ian Smith 2013, 14).

Furthermore, as Smith shows, black face make up in court masques and on the public stage was not only created cosmetically (with soot from charcoal) but prosthetically (with leather gloves on hands and fine black gauze draping the face). Like the handkerchief, 'the black body in the early modern theatre is the product of artistic and artisanal creation – conceived, sewed, dyed' (Ian Smith, 22). We should bear this in mind when we look at the language in which Othello is described and the language in which the handkerchief is described.

Women

Shakespeare alters another significant detail in Cinthio: the relationship the corporal (Shakespeare's Cassio) has to women. In addition to his employment of the sewing lady, Cinthio's corporal also pays a prostitute. It is while he is leaving her house one evening that the ensign attacks him. This is the only mention of the prostitute. When the ensign stages an overseeing episode, as in Shakespeare, all we are told is that 'while chatting of quite other matters than the Lady [Disdemona]', the ensign 'laughed heartily, and displaying great surprise, he moved his head about and gestured with his hands, acting as if he were listening to marvels' (379). This is part of Cinthio's stress on the ensign's acting abilities; the prostitute is not the subject of dialogue here, nor does she enter unexpectedly as in Shakespeare.

By conflating two female characters, Shakespeare obviously reduces the need for two boy actors when one will do. But there may be more to it than that. He gives Cassio's girlfriend the resonant name, Bianca (= white) – resonant in a play which investigates stereotypes associated with the colours black/white.

Bianca is designated 'courtesan' in the dramatis personae of the 1623 Folio (the 1622 quarto does not have a list of the characters). Both texts refer to her as 'Bianca' in stage direction and speech prefixes. This is probably how Shakespeare thought of her – the Folio's dramatis personae list is unlikely to come from Shakespeare's pen. In the early modern period, the word 'courtesan' referred to a woman who had lost her virginity as well as to one who was paid for professional sexual services. There was simply no available noun to indicate a loyal loving unmarried woman who had had sex with one man (Wayne, 192). Iago reinforces our impression of Bianca as a sex worker: he describes her as 'a housewife that by selling her desires / Buys herself breads and clothes' (4.1.95–6). By this time in the play, however, I am not inclined to trust anything Iago says; and, as we shall see, one of the play's projects is to ask us to question the basis on which we know, or think we know, self-evident truths.

For despite the fact that Iago and Cassio talk about Bianca as a whore, she acts more like a girlfriend. She waits for Cassio to come and have supper with her; she embroiders for him; she distinguishes herself from Cassio's 'hobbyhorse [prostitute]' (4.1.153). In fact, this last reference shows her distinctly upset at the thought that Cassio might be paying for sex. However, Cassio describes her as a 'bauble [plaything]' at 4.1.134, and when she exits the scene in distress his instinct is simply to shut her up:

Iago.   After her, after her!
Cassio.   Faith, I must, she'll rail in the streets else.
                                              (4.1.159–60)

We noted above the play's serial silencing of women: Emilia, Bianca, Desdemona. (Emilia is told to hold her tongue, Desdemona is suffocated, and Cassio exits in order to quieten Bianca.) But the point I want to make here concerns the women's identities. Three women in this play are called 'whore'. We know that one (Desdemona) is not unchaste. What do we know about the other two? Production history is relevant here: contrast the high-class lady-in-waiting of the BBC production with the tousled strumpet of the Oliver Parker film (1995) and the Janet Suzman Johannesburg production (filmed 1988). These productions (and others) show different directors' interpretations of the play's language: they have assessed Iago's descriptions of Bianca, and the attitudes implicit in Bianca's language, and found reasons to believe or disbelieve one.

Location, location, location

Cinthio's action has little to do with Venice although his story begins and ends there. Shakespeare makes much of the contrast between Venice (famous city-state, home of law and order) and Cyprus (island of Aphrodite, the goddess of love and beauty who rose from the foam there (Greek, *aphros* – hence her Greek name; the Romans know her as Venus)). This contrast is not an unusual structure in Shakespeare's plays, especially in his comedies which consistently contrast two locations and the attitudes and atmospheres associated with each. Think of the repressive, punitive court in Act One of *As You Like It* versus the pastoral Forest of Arden, home of free speech, whither the characters escape in Act Two; or the court world of public masculine duty and responsibility in *1 Henry IV* versus the feminized world of the Eastcheap tavern where, for Falstaff and his associates, hours are cups of sack, minutes are capons, and clocks the tongues of bawds (*1 Henry IV*, 1.2.6–8).

We might ask ourselves: in what way is Venice important to the action of this play? Is it necessary? After all, Verdi's opera (1887) manages perfectly well without it, opening in Cyprus. It is worth looking at another play with a Venetian setting, *The Merchant of Venice*. One critic offers a sophisticated entrée to this comparative topic, with a number of pithy soundbite sentences that would make good essay topics. For instance: 'In *The Merchant of Venice* the law must be protected because it guarantees commerce; in *Othello* Othello must be protected because he guarantees commerce'; 'Iago and Shylock represent a challenge to Venice precisely because they exploit the structure of Venice' (Holderness, Potter and Turner, 204). As can be seen from these quotations, the critical focus is on the relationship between the self and the state. The commercial urban space of Venice is at odds with the heroic romantic background and aspirations of Othello beside whom Venice seems prosaic and pragmatic. We will return to this topic in Chapter 2 when we consider the question of genre. Is it the move from the city to the island that partly changes the genre of *Othello*? Are Iago and Othello already in different genres, with Iago a cunning city-type and Othello an epic warrior?

Acting Othello

Shakespeare's first Othello was one of the most famous actors of the Elizabethan stage, Richard Burbage. Richard was part of an Elizabethan theatrical dynasty: his father, James

Burbage, built the first permanent Elizabethan playhouse, called the Theatre, in Shoreditch on the North side of the River Thames, and his elder brother, Cuthbert, was also an actor. Born in 1568, Richard played leading parts for Shakespeare's company in the 1590s and 1600s. A list of certain and probable roles includes Hieronimo in Thomas Kyd's *The Spanish Tragedy*, Romeo, Richard III, Shylock, Henry V, Brutus, Hamlet, Othello, Macbeth, King Lear, as well as Ben Jonson's comic charlatans, Volpone in *Volpone* (1606) and Subtle in *The Alchemist* (1612); Burbage also played lead roles in other Jonson comedies and tragedies. He continued to act until the year of his death in 1619. His roles were long – over 800 lines – at a time when a lead part was typically 600 lines.

We know and/or deduce Burbage's roles from cast lists in printed plays, from the commonplace book (notebook) of the Middle Temple lawyer, John Manningham, and from manuscript poems written at Richard's death. One poem in particular, 'A Funeral Elegy on the Death of the Famous Actor Richard Burbage ... 1619', is particularly helpful in listing roles. But caveat: it exists in several manuscript versions; the longer and more detailed versions include lines that are almost certainly forged by the Victorian researcher John Payne Collier. The Red Alert detail is that the poem mentions Burbage acting in plays that belonged to five acting companies (no Elizabethan actor has been found acting for more than one company at the same time). Collating the manuscripts in 1881, one critic noticed the coincidence with which the seven manuscript discoveries happened to increase 'in interest and importance from the comparatively colourless version in eighty-two lines, published in 1825, to the final poem, full of names and striking allusions, and extending to 124 lines' (Ingleby, 174). Internet sources do not distinguish between the different versions or examine the provenance of the version they print. We can have confidence in only the shortest (less detailed) version.

When the writer of 'A Funeral Elegy on the death of the

Famous Actor Richard Burbage' surveys Burbage's career, what he praises most is Burbage's ability to portray grief. He even calls on the dead actor to express the writer's own grief at Burbage's death:

> He's gone, that could the best both limn [paint]
> And act my grief ...
> For none but Tully [the Roman orator, Marcus Tullius
>   Cicero] Tully's praise can tell
> And as he could, no man act so well
> This part of sorrow.

> > (Ingleby, 180; I have modernized the spelling)

Elizabethan acting is often thought to have been less naturalistic than the kind we value today. It may well have been. We need only think back to acting styles in films of the 1950s, or in silent movies, to see how exaggerated their mode appears to us now. This does not mean the style was unnatural in its time. The elegy on Burbage's death repeatedly emphasizes the actor's ability to portray emotions naturally: 'so this map *truly to the life* of woe', 'grief's *true picture*' (Ingleby, 177, 180, my italics). The poet singles out the great Shakespeare tragic heroes – Hamlet, Lear and 'the grieved Moor' ('Affected with grief; vexed, afflicted, troubled or distressed in mind'; *OED* 4; Ingleby, 180). These memories accord with Richard Flecknoe's seventeenth-century description of Burbage in terms that we would recognize from twentieth-century 'Method Acting' where the actor *becomes* the character. Burbage was 'a delightful Proteus [the Greek god Proteus was able to change shape] so wholly transforming himself into his Part, and putting off himself with his Cloathes, as he never (not so much as in the Tyring-house) assum'd himself again until the Play was ended' (Chambers, vol. 4, 370).

Acting Desdemona

An Oxford spectator felt the same about the boy actor who played Desdemona. Shakespeare's acting company, the King's Men performed *Othello* on tour in Oxford in 1610. The Oxford academic, Henry Jackson, wrote a letter in Latin to a friend, describing the actor's effective performance of the dying Desdemona. He praised the actor who had moved the spectators throughout the play 'yet moved [us] more after she was dead, when, lying on her bed, she entreated the pity of the spectators by her very countenance' (reprinted in Riverside Shakespeare, 1852). So convinced is Jackson by the boy-Desdemona's performance that he refers to the boy as 'she' throughout (Latin forces him to choose a consistent gendered grammatical form for his description, either masculine or feminine, unlike English which permits hybrids such as my 'boy-Desdemona').

What the boy actor may have lacked in the role, however, was stamina. Desdemona is a long and varied part: feisty and eloquent in the Senate; anxious but publicly playful on the quayside in Cyprus; rapturous in reunion with her husband; teasing and insistent in pleading for Cassio's reinstatement; hurt and bewildered when humiliated and hit in public; contemplative and melancholically musical in conversation with Emilia in Act Four; energetic and physical when resisting death in Act Five. The Quarto of 1622 is shorter than its 1623 Folio counterpart by approximately 150 lines; and many of the cuts come in the two major boys' roles – Desdemona and Emilia. Let us explore the possible reasons for these variants.

Publishing *Othello*

Shakespeare had been dead for six years when *Othello* first reached print in 1622 in a small paperback format, a single-play Quarto. The following year it was reprinted as part of the collected plays of Shakespeare, published in a large collector's edition, an imposing Folio format. There are over 1,000 small lexical differences between the two texts. A few passages exist only in the Quarto version, while about 160 lines are unique to the Folio. Here is a sample of the localized variants (references in parentheses are to the line numbers in Honigmann's edition of the play; I have modernized Quarto spellings and made all upper case letters lower case).

Quarto	*Folio*
provulgate	promulgate (1.2.21)
intentively	instinctively (1.3.156)
sighs	kisses (1.3.160)
scorn	storm (1.3.250)
utmost pleasure	very quality (1.3.252)
active instruments	officed instrument (1.3.271)
concern	import (1.3.284)
acerb	bitter (1.3.350)
communicative	conjunctive (1.3.368)
bear all excellency	tire the inginir (2.1.65)
enscerped	ensteeped (2.1.70)
expert	exquisite (2.3.76)
some things	two things (2.3.377)
muttering	mamm'ring (3.3.70)
strongly	soundly (3.3.172)
great clamour	dread clamours (3.3.359)
excellency	execution (3.3.469)
convenient	continuate (3.4.178)
this the noble nature	is this the nature (4.1.265)
part	place (4.2.53)
commission	command (4.2.222)
dispatch	dismiss (4.3.7)
think'st	know'st (5.1.25)
fate hies apace	unblest fate hies (5.1.34)
return	relume (5.2.13)
lodging	loading (5.2.361)

There are also some larger alterations (excisions from Quarto or additions to Folio). Othello's Pontic Sea speech, for instance (3.3.456–64 in Honigmann's edition) exists only in the Folio. In Act Four of Quarto *Othello*, the boy actor of Desdemona does not sing the haunting willow song, and his/her dialogue with Emilia is reduced.

It is hard to know what to make of these cumulative differences. The differences in the list above do not form an obvious pattern; sometimes exotic vocabulary in Quarto is made more familiar in Folio but sometimes it is the other way round. Some of the larger changes have to be considered together. For instance, Emilia dies in the Folio with an action replay of Desdemona's willow song and an explicit reference to it:

What did thy song bode, lady?
Hark, canst thou hear me I will play the swan
And die in music. [*Sings.*] Willow, willow, willow.
— Moor, she was chaste, she loved thee, cruel Moor,
So come my soul to bliss as I speak true!
So speaking as I think, alas, I die.

(5.2.244–9, cited from Honigmann's edition)

Whoever removed Desdemona's song from the Folio version also removed this reference to it so that in the Quarto text Emilia dies as follows:

Moor, she was chaste, she loved thee, cruel Moor.
So come my soul to bliss as I speak true;
So speaking as I think, I die, I die.

(Quarto text, ed. McMillin, 5.2.266–8)

These are the kind of tinkerings that may suggest authorial revision. There is no party-line view of the two texts' origins but current thinking views both of them as legitimate performance scripts prepared and performed at some stage in the history of the King's Men before 1622. The absence of oaths from the Folio text points to a date of post-1606 for this version, since the Statute against Abuses which prohibited swearing and blasphemy on stage was introduced that year.

It is not important to have a theory as to why the texts differ. It is, however, important to know where they differ and to take this into account when forming a critical argument. One strand of *Othello* criticism concerns the silencing of women (I have already mentioned this twice in this chapter). Folio-Emilia has much to say about wives who are prompted to adultery by their husbands' neglect (18 lines not in the Quarto: 4.3.85–102). In the scene before this, Folio-Desdemona swears on her knees that she never has and never will love anyone except Othello (4.2.153–66): these 14 lines are not in the Quarto. In the play's last scene, Folio-Emilia is more vocal in helping to expose Iago. Her lines (and Othello's consequent response) at 5.2.147–50 are not in the Quarto; neither are her Folio lines, prompting the responses of Gratiano and Montano, at 5.2.181–90. It is impossible to resist the conclusion that these changes are connected; and it would be hard to formulate an argument about the women's roles without taking these differences into account.

In making language-based arguments in an essay (and all arguments are language based!) it is important not to mix and match the Quarto/Folio texts. There is one linguistic pattern in the Quarto and a different linguistic pattern in the Folio. A modern editor will make it clear whether the Quarto or the Folio text is the basis of his/her edition. (This information is not always available in older editions or in internet editions.)

If textual variants inform critical arguments, they also affect our sense of theatre. A plaingently musical Desdemona in Folio's Act Four gives the scene a slower tempo than its Quarto counterpart which is more accelerated in dialogue. Is a musical Desdemona more contemplative or more fretful? How is the relationship between the women presented in the longer and shorter versions of this scene? This is, after all, a crucial domestic scene of female bonding and conversation. The innocent atmosphere of female talk was conveyed brilliantly in Trevor Nunn's 1989 Royal Shakespeare Company production; it was cemented when Desdemona opened a locked drawer and the two women shared a guilty treat – a box of chocolates given to Desdemona by Cassio. (See Carol Rutter's chapter on this production's women in *Enter the Body*, 142–77.)

It is noticeable that when early modern playtexts are revised, revisions are often made in Act Four – is this an attempt to accelerate the play's pace as we approach the denouement or to give a major actor a break before a climactic finale? Perhaps the most famous example is in Folio *Hamlet* which removes one of Hamlet's soliloquies; Fortinbras crosses Denmark en route to Poland in 4.4 but Hamlet is not on stage to watch him and hence is not prompted to say 'How all occasions do inform against me, / And spur my dull revenge' (4.4.32ff.). The reasons for Quarto *Othello*'s changes in Act Four may well be practical: waning energy in the boy actor of Desdemona or, more probably, a change of boy actor (from a singing boy to one who could not sing) or some alteration in the existing boy actor which prevented him singing (did his voice break?). A similar vocal issue may have affected the boy who played Viola in *Twelfth Night*. When Viola is shipwrecked in Illyria she plans to offer her services to Count Orsino as a eunuch 'for I can sing / And speak to him in many sorts of music' (2.1.57–8). This plan never materializes. Instead Feste, the fool, is the play's singing character but, unusually, he belongs neither to Orsino's nor to Olivia's court: he commutes between the two. When he is required to sing at Orsino's palace in Act Two he is inconveniently absent. Although we are told that he is 'about the house', the line associates him with Olivia's court ('a fool that the Lady Olivia's father took much delight in'; 2.4.8–13) and Olivia's waiting-woman chastises Feste for his frequent absences from Olivia's court (1.5.1–21). One explanation for all of this is that Viola's was originally a singing role and when the boy actor's voice broke, his songs were transferred to Feste and the plot adapted.

This coincidence – a singing boy actor in *Twelfth Night* whose songs were cut and a singing boy actor in *Othello* whose song is cut – led Ernst Honigmann to conclude that it was the same boy actor in both plays. He therefore places the composition of *Othello* about the same time as *Twelfth Night* in 1601–2. (Previous editors thought – and some still think – that it was written in 1603–4; 1604 is the date of the first recorded performance when the King's Men played before the King at Court in November.) The cut and adapted text of *Othello* reached print in 1622, with a variant version, reflecting the King's Men's text at some other time, following in print a year later.

Textual theories about actors or dramaturgy are not independent of considerations of language: as the parallel columns of Quarto/Folio variants above indicate, when Shakespeare made large changes to do with actors and scenes he could not resist making local lexical changes – what we might call 'tinkering'. These changes, major and minor, affect how we read and see the play. This is the same kind of artistic process as when Shakespeare adapted Cinthio's novella into a five-act play, adding and removing details, providing names, shaping our dramatic perspective. Every decision he made, at every stage, affects the language he and his characters use – as we shall see in the chapters that follow.

CHAPTER ONE

Language and narrative

One of the arguments of this book will be that *Othello* is a play interested in small words: conjunctions ('and', 'but'), adverbs ('yet', 'indeed'), verbs of modality ('shall', 'may', will'), negatives ('never'), adjectives ('honest'), the verb 'to be'. In later sections and chapters I shall look down the linguistic microscope at these small words but I want to begin with a telescopic approach and look at the larger universe that these individual words comprise: narrative. This is, after all, a play in which the hero wins his bride by telling the story of his life (or, in Iago's reductive summary, 'but for bragging and telling her fantastical lies'; 1.3.130; 2.1.221). It is a play which begins with Roderigo's incredulity that Iago should have denied him a narrative, the crucial backstory of Othello and Desdemona's love, elopement and marriage: 'never tell me', he chastises (1.1.1) or, perhaps, asks incredulously (some editors add a question mark). It is a play that ends with a desire for narrative – Othello's 'speak of me as I am' (5.2.340) as he instructs Gratiano (Desdemona's uncle) and the onstage audience how to 'relate' (5.2.339) the tragic events. 'Relate' is, in fact, the play's last word as Gratiano prepares to go 'aboard, and to the state / This heavy act with heavy heart relate' (5.2.369).

But narrative is complicated for many reasons. In the last scene alone we see Emilia's belated determination to 'speak as liberal as the north. / Let heaven and men and devils, let them all, / All, all cry shame against me, yet I'll speak', a determination that leads directly to her death. Othello too talks himself to death. His autobiographical summary ('one that loved not wisely but too well ...'; 5.2.342ff.) may sound, as the twentieth-century critic and poet, T. S. Eliot, puts it, like Othello attempting to cheer himself up (Eliot, 130–1), but it is also an attempt to recuperate his identity in narrative – or rather, in a blending of third-person past-tense narrative ('a malignant and a turbanned Turk / Beat a Venetian') with first-person present-tense drama ('I took by th'throat the circumcised dog / And smote him – thus'; 5.2.351–4). We will consider the overlapping of narrative with drama later; here I simply want to draw attention to the problems of presenting identity linguistically. Iago's refusal to engage in narrative may be a recognition of this difficulty:

> Demand me nothing. What you know, you know.
> From this time forth I never will speak word.
>
> (5.2.300–1)

Critics (and medics) often comment on the impossibility of Desdemona continuing to speak after suffocation. But this physiological impossibility is paralleled by a narrative impossibility – Othello's 'speak of me as I am'. What does it mean to speak of someone as they are, especially in this play where Iago has fractured the verb 'to be' (Morgan, 92–106)? Iago confesses in Act One that 'I am not what I am' (1.1.64), a rupture of correspondence that can stand in for the whole play where white becomes black, loyalty seems infidelity and honesty masks betrayal. How to speak of someone as they are is a question Shakespeare confronts again and again, both in tragic drama (see the brief summaries of Hamlet by Fortinbras at the end of *Hamlet*, of Brutus by Mark Antony at the end of *Julius Caesar*, of Coriolanus by Tullus Aufidius at the end of *Coriolanus*, and of Cleopatra by Octavius Caesar at the end of *Antony and Cleopatra*) and in tragic narrative (think, for instance, of the attempts by father and husband to speak of Lucrece after her suicide in Shakespeare's early narrative poem, *The Rape of Lucrece*, published in 1594). For now, let us try to unpack this narrative problem by looking at some of *Othello*'s inset narratives – moments of story-telling onstage.

Story-telling

The first set piece is Othello's account to the Senate in 1.3. The piece has a practical function – it covers the time until Desdemona arrives, as Othello explicitly acknowledges – but it also works as a legal presentation of a case:

> And till she come ...
> So justly to your grave ears I'll present
> How I did thrive in this fair lady's love
> And she in mine.

> (1.3.124–8)

Given that 'present' is a legal term, meaning 'lay before a court' as one editor glosses it (Honigmann 1.3.125n) and that 'justly' means 'faithfully', Othello here promises to tell the truth, the whole truth and nothing but the truth. My use of the noun 'account' at the start of this paragraph is not accidental: in many works of literature, *re*counting one's life and actions is equated with *ac*counting for one's life and actions.

Othello's speech is a crucial moment in a scene of narrative opposition and balancing. Let us recap what has happened in the scene so far.

Brabantio accuses Othello of having bewitched his daughter (1.3.61–5); Othello corrects the terminology, promising to explain how he 'won' Brabantio's daughter (94). Brabantio interrupts, reiterating his accusation of a one-sided occurrence: magic and theft (104–7). However, the First Senator is aware that every story has two sides. The marriage can be the result of coercion, as Brabantio has presented it. The First Senator asks Othello:

> Did you by indirect and forced courses
> Subdue and poison this young maid's affections?

(1.3.112–13)

Or the marriage can be a story of reciprocal love:

> Or came it by request and such fair question
> As soul to soul affordeth?

(1.3.114–15)

We are offered a view from the outsider's perspective (Brabantio) or from the insiders' (the married couple). But because these insiders are not one but two – a couple – Othello further acknowledges that the two parties involved in the marriage will have two stories. He tells his own version, after which Desdemona is offered the opportunity to tell hers – 'let her witness it' (1.3.171).

We might note, by the way, that this structure of bifurcation, division, duality is continued when Desdemona introduces her narrative as a story of 'divided duty', in which she weighs loyalty to her father versus loyalty to her new husband, choosing the latter as her mother had done before her. This is a play that is very aware of the potential for all meaning or response or interpretation to have two perspectives. Every story can be told in multiple ways, making it more than one story.

Othello's story of the wooing changes the tone and pace of the scene. Up to this point the scene has been characterized by its urgency. We have had exclamation ('My daughter, O my daughter!'; 60), accusation (61–5, 72), and interruption (75–6): at line 75 the Duke asks Othello 'What in your own part can you say to this?' but it is *Brabantio* who responds

'Nothing, but this is so', not giving Othello a chance to defend himself. When Othello finally addresses the Senate, it is the longest speech so far.

Having established the context, we can now turn to the speech. It is formal in its opening:

> Most potent, grave, and reverend signiors,
> My very noble and approved good masters

(1.3.77–8)

It is rhetorically balanced:

> That I have ta'en away this old man's daughter
> It is most true; true, I have married her.

(1.3.79–80)

(The structure in these two lines is chiastic. *Chiasmus* is the rhetorical term for inversion, the sequence in which the order of words in one clause is reversed in the second. In this example, the inversion is verb (ta'en away), adjective (true) // adjective (true), verb (married).)

It disavows rhetorical ability, as the best orators do. 'Rude am I in my speech', apologizes Othello (82), the early modern equivalent of our pre-emptive strike, 'Unaccustomed as I am to public speaking' ... This negative warm up ('rude am I'; 'little blest' (83); 'little shall I grace my cause' (89)) is followed by a pivotal contrasting conjunction, 'yet'. In other words, 'I'm not capable of speaking – but I'll do it':

> Yet, by your gracious patience,
> I will a round unvarnished tale deliver
> Of my whole course of love.

(1.3.90–2)

Unlike the story of witchcraft told by his accuser, Othello's story is one of reciprocation:

So justly to your ears I'll present
How I did thrive in this fair lady's love
And she in mine.

(1.3.126–8)

Othello's speech functions, in film terms, as a flashback. It tells us the *story* that precedes the *plot* (plot is what we see drama- tized in the five acts on stage; story is the larger narrative that precedes this – the murder of old King Hamlet, for instance, or the exile of Prospero from Milan in *The Tempest*). In Oliver Parker's film of *Othello* (1995) this speech is indeed a flashback. The camera captures a sunlit scene of a canopied outdoor gathering, Desdemona eagerly straining to overhear Othello's tales to her father. When the couple are alone together and Othello notices Desdemona weeping, he wipes her tears with a strawberry-embroidered handkerchief.

Othello's narrative of life and love begins (like Viola's narrative of her life and love in a play very close in date to *Othello, Twelfth Night*) with the father. It is Brabantio who set this story in motion: 'Her father loved me, oft invited me, / Still questioned me the story of my life' (129–30). The story of Othello's life starts with the play's longest sentence, at least in most modern editions. The two earliest printings, Quarto and Folio, break up the flow by inserting full stops – one full stop in the quarto, three in the Folio. However, their punctuation is misleading by either early modern or modern standards and the punctuation in modern editions (such as the one from which I quote, edited by Honigmann) makes both phrasing and sense clearer with their use of semi-colons and commas:

I ran it through, even from my boyish days
To th' very moment that he bade me tell it,
Wherein I spake of most disastrous chances,
Of moving accidents by flood and field,
Of hair-breadth scapes i'th' imminent deadly breach,
Of being taken by the insolent foe
And sold to slavery; of my redemption thence

And portance in my travailous history;
Wherein of antres vast and deserts idle,
Rough quarries, rocks and hills whose heads touch heaven
It was my hint to speak – such was my process –
And of the cannibals that each other eat,
The Anthropophagi, and men whose heads
Do grow beneath their shoulders.

(1.3.133–46)

This sentence is essentially a list. Lists are acoustically alluring, as our contemporary predilection for one-person shows in which an actor reads out the telephone directory demonstrates. But Othello's is no ordinary list. It provides the most exotic and multisyllabic vocabulary in the play so far: 'travailous', 'antres', 'Anthropophagi'. And it presents a romance tale of danger, capture, slavery, rescue.

This romance tale is not unlike Prospero's to his daughter Miranda at the start of *The Tempest* (1.2). Prospero is in exile from his dukedom in Milan, having escaped with Miranda when she was aged two; now, twelve years later, he sees fit to tell her the story of his life. But whereas Prospero's autobiography threatens to bore Miranda or send her to sleep (she is thrice reprimanded for inattention and is only slowly drawn into the narrative), Othello's has an immediate effect on his auditor: Desdemona is eager to hear more: 'She'd come again and with a greedy ear / Devour up my discourse' (150–1). The physical vocabulary of appetite and consumption ('greedy', 'devour') not only materializes the idea of story-telling (stories are something that can be eaten) but associates Desdemona with unladylike appetite and desires (early modern women were not supposed to have physical appetites for anything).

The narrative also creates contradictory emotions:

She swore in faith 'twas strange, 'twas passing strange,
'Twas pitiful, 'twas wondrous pitiful;
She wished she had not heard it, yet ...

(161–3)

The narrative has a somatic effect: we hear of Desdemona's tears and of her sighs/kisses (1.3.160). The Quarto and Folio texts vary here: in the former, Desdemona gives Othello a 'world of sighs', in the Folio 'a world of kisses'. (The flashback in the Oliver Parker film turns the Folio reading into onscreen action, depicting a sexually impulsive Desdemona.)

We also see here something that will be important to the play, the reciprocity of responses between tale-teller and listener. Othello notes his auditor's eager reaction to his story ('which I observing'), speaks to her alone, is requested to tell more tales, 'did consent', and so a different reciprocity develops:

> She loved me for the dangers I had passed
> And I loved her that she did pity them.

> (1.3.168–9)

Othello concludes with a crisp summary ('This only is the witchcraft I have used') before Desdemona enters: 'Here comes the lady, let her witness it' (169–70). 'Witness' is another legal term: i.e. 'let her give her evidence'. We will now hear another version of the story.

Two items merit note here. The first is that, in describing the effect on Desdemona, Othello restages the effect – on us. We are wooed; we are drawn in; we are persuaded. It is an effect the play will restage again (and again), showing not just Desdemona's seduction by narrative but narrative as seduction.

The second is that this scene is not about one set of contradictory stories (Othello as magician versus Othello as wooer) but about two: it begins with two contradictory accounts of the Turkish fleet. These are entirely separate narratives (a political invasion, a domestic invasion) but, as an audience adjudicating each pair of stories, we cannot help but notice the ways in which they coincide or bifurcate. Let us turn our attention to the dialogue that precedes Othello's accusation and defence.

Contradiction

Act 1, scene 3 begins mid-debate with the Duke trying to evaluate two inconsistent reports: 'there is no composition in these news / That gives them credit' (in Shakespeare's day, 'news' was a plural noun, hence the Duke's 'these' and 'them'; 1.3.1–2). His perplexity is caused by the Senate's receipt of two letters reporting a threatening Turkish fleet; in one letter the fleet comprises 107 galleys, in another 140. Despite this inconsistency, the letters agree on the crucial detail of the fleet's destination: Cyprus. But a sailor now enters and announces that 'the Turkish preparation makes for Rhodes' (1.3.15–16). This news causes perplexity. The first narrative, despite its inconsistency in numbers, is logical, politically and strategically: Cyprus, as a Venetian outpost, an island on the border of East and West, is vulnerable to threats from the Ottomans. The second narrative makes no sense at all – 'This cannot be, / By no assay of reason' (1.3.21).

In fact both stories turn out to be true. A messenger enters with an update: the Turks have received naval reinforcements at Rhodes and, with 30 more ships, openly ('with frank appearance') 'do re-stem / Their backward course, ... / ... toward Cyprus' (1.3.38–40). In this episode, two contradictory stories are quickly resolved.

The scene now moves to the two wooing stories: Brabantio's narrative of a scared, reluctant, 'never bold', daughter; Othello's alternative narrative that she was 'half the wooer' (Brabantio's phrase at 176). The two episodes are parallel – evidence is adjudicated – but not identical. The Duke proceeds by intuition, which happens to be proved correct. But a pattern has been introduced: the contradictory narrative.

Doubled and contradictory narratives are not confined to this scene. The play gives us a further account of the wooing. In Act Three Desdemona talks of 'Michael Cassio / That came a-wooing with you' (3.3.70–1). In the same scene Iago disingenuously asks Othello 'Did Michael Cassio, when you wooed my lady, / Know of your love?', only to be told 'O yes, and went between us very oft' (3.3.94–5, 100). How does this square with Othello's Senate narrative of delivering his autobiography to a single audience member, one who sped through her household tasks to devour his stories, one who wept and sighed (or kissed) in response? A Desdemona who offers explicit romantic encouragement needs no go-between – 'She ... / Bade me, if I had a friend that loved her, / I should but teach him how to tell my story / And that would woo her. Upon this hint I spake' (1.3.164–7). An Othello who is invited repeatedly into the household by Brabantio needs no go-between.

Othello later offers two contradictory narratives of the handkerchief ('her first remembrance from the Moor', says Emilia at 3.3.295; ''twas my first gift' confirms Othello at 3.3.439). But this first gift has two narratives of origin. In one story, the handkerchief has a matrilineal origin, in the other, a patrilineal. Both narratives are foregrounded. In 3.4, Othello tells Desdemona that his mother received the handkerchief from an Egyptian enchantress. Its magical property was to make the owner desirable to her husband. The fabric was woven from hallowed silkworms, and it was 'dyed in mummy, which the skilful / Conserved of maidens' hearts' (3.4.76–7). Desdemona's reaction is not unexpected – 'Is it true?' (3.4.77). In Act Five, however, we get a different story. Defending his murder of his wife, offering the proof of her adultery, Othello cites the handkerchief:

> It was a handkerchief, an antique token
> My father gave my mother.

> (5.2.214–15)

Clearly both stories cannot be correct. Either the Egyptian charmer gave it to Othello's mother or his father did. One can use the narratives' structural placings to argue that the story in Act Three is designed as a warning (and therefore untrue) or one can argue that by Act Five Othello is a crazed murderer (and so this story is untrue). But Shakespeare gives us no clear means to adjudicate the likelihood of one story being more plausible than the other. We are in the same position as Othello when he does not know what to think (3.3.387–8). The handkerchief, woven anew with every story threaded into it, becomes an emblem for the way narrative works in this play. Iago is not the only one to spin a yarn. The play puts story-telling under pressure in a number of ways, exploring its potential for alternative interpretations while at times making it impossible for us to interpret at all.

Believing stories

Other narratives in the play are more clearly legible as false or fictitious. But what is not in doubt is their narrative power and effect. In Act Three, Iago offers the first of his potential proofs of Desdemona's adultery when he recounts an episode where he and Cassio shared a bed. The bedsharing may or may not be fictitious (Russ McDonald reminds us that 'Iago uses whatever he finds'; McDonald, 187) but Cassio's dream, in which he re-enacts sharing a bed with Desdemona, presumably is.

> I lay with Cassio lately;
> And, being troubled with a raging tooth,
> I could not sleep. There are a kind of men
> So loose of soul that in their sleeps will mutter
> Their affairs – one of this kind is Cassio.
> In sleep I heard him say 'Sweet Desdemona,
> Let us be wary, let us hide our loves,'
> And then, sir, would he gripe and wring my hand,
> Cry 'O sweet creature!' and then kiss me hard,
> As if he plucked up kisses by the roots
> That grew upon my lips, lay his leg o'er my thigh,
> And sigh, and kiss, and then cry 'Cursed fate
> That gave thee to the Moor!'

(3.3.416–28)

(An aside: Trevor Nunn's Royal Shakespeare Company *Othello* of 1989 (filmed 1990) cleverly prepared this moment. In 2.3, Iago sat on the army-barracks bed in which Cassio lay down to recover after his drunkenness; Cassio writhed in a sexual dream and moved his leg 'o'er [Iago's] thigh', cueing Iago's later opportunistic narrative embroidery of the event.)

Having recounted the episode to Othello, Iago tries to undo the narrative ('Nay, this was but his dream'; 3.3.429), but as Frank Kermode notes (in Riverside, 1200), the play is full of uncancelled suggestions and Othello not surprisingly responds with unquestioning acceptance: 'But this denoted a foregone conclusion' (3.3.430). (The phrase sounds modern but it is slightly different from our use, referring to previous ('foregone') occasions ('conclusion').) The point is that Othello reacts as the senators did not; they puzzled over logic and illogic, keeping their options open.

Othello's readiness to conclude paves the way for Iago to redefine this narrative not as a dream but as evidence which can support less tangible evidence:

> And this may help to thicken other proofs
> That do demonstrate thinly.

> (3.3.431–3)

The slippage of language and logic here is extraordinary. The dream he has tried to distance from evidence ('this was *but* his dream') now becomes supporting evidence; if it bolsters '*other* proofs', that means that the dream is also 'proof' – and, by implication, *strong* proof since the other proofs with which it is contrasted are *thin* proofs.

'I say' and 'yet'

Perhaps most interesting in this context is the play's use of the verb 'to say'. Characters do not simply say something, but frequently say that they are saying, or have said, something. 'I say it is not lost' protests Desdemona (3.4.87). Does this mean the same as 'it is not lost' (which is what she said in her preceding line)? 'I say, put money in thy purse' says Iago in 1.3, a few lines after saying simply 'put money in thy purse' (1.3.342, 340). Earlier he has ushered Roderigo offstage: 'Away, I say' (2.3.153). In these instances, 'I say' means no more than 'I repeat'. Less clear is Othello's use of the verb when Iago tells him that Venetian women 'do let God see the pranks / They dare not show their husbands' (3.3.205–6). Othello responds, 'Dost thou say so?' (3.3.208) . This could be an expression of incredulity (i.e. 'are you kidding?'); certainly Iago takes it that way when, in his next line, he offers confirmation of his truism about Venetian women's deceptions with an example ('She did deceive her father, marrying you'). But Othello's question might equally mean that he views the fact of Iago's articulation as an intensifier (the statement is to be believed because Iago has actually said it) or as evidence of Iago's conviction of what he describes (Iago must believe it because he has gone as far as to say it). Whatever its precise meaning, in all of these instances the phrase works to reinforce meaning.

In the Senate scene Othello volunteers to narrate his romance with Desdemona. The Duke encourages him: 'Say it, Othello' (1.3.128). One editor rightly points out that this is 'an unusual turn of phrase, not quite the same as "speak"' (Honigmann ed., *Othello*, 1.3.128n). But it is not unusual for the *play*, which takes speech as proof. A later version of Othello, the jealous husband Leontes in Shakespeare's *The Winter's Tale*, turns his wife into an adulteress by the sheer act of accusation:

> I have said
> She's an adult'ress; I have said with whom.

(2.1.87–8)

But, as the Duke in *Othello* cautions Brabantio in the senate scene, 'To vouch this is no proof' (1.3.107). The play needs (but lacks) this voice of reason later in Cyprus when Othello starts taking statements for proof. The Duke's simple piece of proverbial wisdom (see 1.3.107n) is the opposition we long to hear offered to Iago. (And thinking back to the question we posed about location in the Introduction – would it matter if we omitted Venice? – we may here see one possible answer. Venice provides logic; Cyprus operates on emotion.)

What does 'I say' mean when it reappears in Iago's mouth after Othello's demand for ocular proof? Iago begins as if assessing the practicalities of an administrative task:

> It were a tedious difficulty, I think,
> To bring them to that prospect.
>
> (3.3.400–1)

He concludes as if doing Othello a favour – as if the office worker has hit on a solution:

> But yet, I say,
> If imputation and strong circumstances
> Which lead directly to the door of truth
> Will give you satisfaction, you may have't.
>
> (3.3.408–10)

'I say' now has the force of 'I promise'. The word has acquired new significance: no longer mere repetition, it offers proof. This is also its implication in Act Four when Iago hypothesizes to Othello: 'What if I had said I had seen him do you wrong?' (4.1.24). This is a bit of a mouthful for an actor and Honigmann is surely right to suggest that on both occurrences 'I had' should be elided to 'I'd' (see his note on this passage in his edition, 4.1.24n). But Shakespeare could have avoided the problem with a variant line, an easier line, a trochaic pentameter: 'What if I had seen him do you wrong?' (A trochee, with one stressed and one unstressed syllable, is the inverse of the iamb which has an unstressed syllable followed by a stressed syllable. Trochaic lines often omit the last unstressed syllable, as in my example here.) But Iago gets mileage out of the verb 'say'. This is his regular tactic – to alter the meaning of small words. It is how he leads Othello 'by th'nose' (1.3.400).

Having first articulated the difficulty of providing ocular proof, Iago introduces his solution (above) with 'But yet' (3.3.408). Like Cleopatra, 'I do not like "but yet"' (*Antony and Cleopatra* 2.5.50). 'Yet' is another of his manipulative small words. Earlier in this scene he has told Othello 'I speak not yet of proof' (3.3.199). How carefully, subtly different is this from 'I speak not of proof'; the adverb implies that proof is available, does indeed exist. By the end of the scene, when Iago introduces the topic of the handkerchief, he can say, 'It speaks against her with the other proofs' (3.3.444), obscuring the fact that there have been no other proofs, only linguistic tricks. And when he says 'But yet' at line 408 the phrase carefully contrasts with the preceding sentiments in which he said that catching Desdemona *in flagrante* would be difficult; the contrastive force of 'but yet' indicates that the difficulty is about to be overcome.

As the scene progresses, his use of the adverb becomes vertiginous:

Nay, **yet** be wise, **yet** we see nothing done,
She may be honest **yet**.

(3.3.435–6, my emphasis)

The Quarto substitutes 'but' for the first 'yet'. Honigmann points out that the Folio sequence, with three *yet*s in two lines, forces emphasis on the third: 'She may be honest – yet [i.e. even if not for long]' (Honigmann ed., 3.3.435n). The word bears all the weight of Iago's implied sexual scepticism.

Iago's solution, however, is linguistically paradoxical: he will offer circumstantial evidence ('imputation and strong circumstances') as if it is 'truth'. But it is not 'truth' to which he offers to lead Othello, just 'the *door* of truth' (my italics). Iago, as we shall see in Chapter 3, is the play's gatekeeper: he is a character who swears by Janus, the Roman god of doors and thresholds, and who hovers on boundaries (Smith 2005, 68). This may be part of the antireligious associations of Iago's language (critics frequently note that 'I am not what I am' (1.1.64) is the opposite of God's declaration 'I am that I am' in Exodus 3.14). Iago haunts doorways and his 'door of truth' leads to destruction but it is Christ who is the door (in some translations: the gate) through which men are saved (John 10:9).

Iago's liminal image, used here as a metaphor, cues literal associations in Othello's and our minds (as it is presumably meant to) – we are not at the door of truth but at the bedroom door. Othello is promised the satisfaction of knowledge and certainty when he sees or imagines the couple receiving sexual satisfaction (the word 'satisfied' occurs three times in 3.3.393–7). But given the voyeuristic implication of Othello's peeping at the threshold is it cognitive or sexual satisfaction that Iago promises?

Undoing narrative

Iago does no more than utter a word; it expands associatively, implicatively, and Othello fills in the gaps. Iago then tries to undo the narrative, often quite bluntly, usually quite truthfully:

> I do beseech you,
> Though I perchance am vicious in my guess
> – As I confess it is my nature's plague
> To spy into abuses, and oft my jealousy
> Shapes faults that are not – that your wisdom
> From one that so imperfectly conceits
> Would take no notice.

(3.3.147–53)

There is an abundance of true statements here: he is vicious, he is envious, he makes things up, he imagines things. But as Shakespeare tells us elsewhere, what is done cannot be undone, in words or associations any more than in deeds. Denying that Cassio is guilty raises the possibility that he is (this is what psychologists call the psychology of negation). A negative expands to become a positive: 'I cannot think it / That he [Cassio] would steal away so guilty-like / Seeing you coming' (3.3.38–40). Having described Cassio's dream of sex with Desdemona, Iago reassures Othello: 'Nay, this was but his dream' (3.3.429). To insist that it was only a dream paradoxically makes possible Othello's view that it was not. The human mind receives suggestions from both positive and negative phrasing; either way the associations cannot be cancelled.

Antony Sher commented on this when he played Iago at the Royal Shakespeare Company in 2004. He noticed that Iago

> urges Othello to doubt his words: 'Say they are vile and false?' [3.3.139]. Later in the scene, he says, 'Let me be thought too busy [meddlesome] in my fears [suspicions] – / As worthy cause I have to fear I am –' [3.3.257–8]. All this is *true*. In a curious way, he is being 'honest Iago'.
>
> (Sher, 63)

Truth becomes deception. Iago's profession is to uphold the sign – as ensign-bearer he carries the troop's sign or standard (Lucking, 113). But, as architect and manipulator of the plot, Iago's role is that of de-signer: he sabotages Othello's trust in the relation between name and identity – 'Her name, that was as fresh / As Dian's visage, is now begrimed and black' (3.3.389–90).

Iago's tactic of planting and cancelling suggestions is visible at the micro level of the word or phrase, as we have been exploring in this chapter. But it also happens at the level of narrative. In Act Two, Othello twice asks Iago to answer the question 'who began this [the fray]', 'who began't' (2.3.174,

213). Montano repeats Othello's request, telling Iago not to deliver 'more or less than truth' (2.3.215). Iago obeys with a narrative of events which is, in many ways, exemplary. It is a straightforward subject-verb-object narration, an account with textbook clarity:

> Thus it is, general.
> Montano and myself being in speech,
> There comes a fellow crying out for help
> And Cassio following him with determined sword
> To execute upon him. Sir, this gentleman
> Steps in to Cassio, and entreats his pause,
> Myself the crying fellow did pursue,
> Lest by his clamour, as it so fell out,
> The town might fall in fright. He, swift of foot,
> Outran my purpose, and I returned the rather
> For that I heard the clink and fall of swords,
> And Cassio high in oath, which till to-night
> I ne'er might say before. When I came back,
> For this was brief, I found them close together
> At blow and thrust, even as again they were
> When you yourself did part them.
> More of this matter cannot I report.

> (2.3.220–36)

There are few details not related to the immediate occurrence he has been asked to describe. There is one significant addition – he had never before seen Cassio 'high in oath' (but note: he does not say he had never 'seen' this but that he never had reason to 'say' this before); this addition is designed (apparently) to exculpate Cassio. But the details have the opposite effect (as of course, they were designed to have).

Othello responds, 'I know, Iago / Thy honesty and love doth mince this matter, / Making it light to Cassio' (2.3.242–4). Iago's laconic narrative has been interpreted as a cover up; Othello fills in the gaps.

Story-telling, like drama, relies on auditors filling in gaps. Narrative and mimetic presentation do not occur in real time. Speakers and writers streamline, omit, imply, edit; auditors complete the story by filling in the lacunae. This, in fact, is how all perception works. In hearing, auditors do not receive every sound transmitted by the speaker but fill in gaps according to logic (deafness is when the gaps outnumber the received words, making the auditor incapable of completing the sense). In night driving, the brain connects remarkably little visual data into a road, a bend, a hill. So too, in fiction: between, for example, a novel's chapter in which a nineteenth-century hero is sentenced to death and a chapter which describes the aftermath of his hanging, we supply a scene of execution.

For many critics, literature is about this relationship between what is present in the text and what is absent from it, a relationship that it is the responsibility of the reader to negotiate, providing continuity and connection (at the most basic level: of character), coordinating viewpoints, and bridging gaps. Tangents and diversions are transformed, fragments joined, blanks filled in. Reading is about turning parts into wholes; it 'trigger[s] synthesizing operations in the reader's mind' (Iser, 66).

Iago is well aware of this. In today's terminology, we would say that Iago is a cognitive psychologist. (Cognitive psychologists study how people think and perceive.) Iago knows how perception works generally and how Othello responds specifically. Othello cannot tolerate gaps; he hastens to fill them in. He tells Iago that 'to be once in doubt / Is once to be resolved' (3.3.182–3). Presumably this is why Iago engineers the kind of plot he does, relying on incomplete sentences and tantalizing suspensions of reaction.

The temptation scene of 3.3 is a superb example of Iago's tactics. It begins, after Desdemona's exit, with the half line, 'My noble lord ...' (3.3.93). Iago addresses Othello but fails to continue, prompting Othello's encouragement, 'What dost thou say?' Later, Iago's casually dismissive 'but for a satisfaction of my thought, / No further harm' (3.3.96–7) leads

Othello to inquire about the 'thought'; Othello's frustration is fuelled by Iago's subsequent echoes and evasions. Iago's gaps are everywhere, not just in words but in silence.

And when Iago places Othello on stage to oversee (not overhear) a staged pantomime, Othello supplies the dialogue: 'Now he denies it'; 'Now he importunes him'; 'now he begins the story'; 'Now he tells how she plucked him to my chamber' (4.1.113, 114, 131, 140–1). Once again, he fills in the gaps.

Audiences and gaps

In 2009 the actor Simon Russell Beale addressed the topic of gap-filling in a lecture to the British Psychoanalytic Society. For him, acting is 'three-dimensional literary criticism' and actors 'lead the audience through a detailed thought-through argument or series of arguments'. To this end, 'it is essential … to clarify and distil the line of thought in an individual character's head before one begins to explore other emotional areas'. But he adds an important caveat which allows the actor to play gaps – and the audience to fill them in:

> There are times when, after narrowing options as far as possible, the most valuable course of action in performance is to leave things be, as it were to let motive, intention, a particular emotional state, remain muddied, even self-contradictory. In any case, the observer, each individual audience member, determines what is seen and understood – a sort of theatrical uncertainty principle.
>
> (Beale, theatre programme)

Productions often exploit this potential for ambiguity. Richard McCabe describes how his Iago concluded Michael Attenborough's production for the Royal Shakespeare Company in 1999:

Our production ended in a tableau, with the three dead bodies in the foreground and myself at the rear of the stage, heavily guarded and with my back to the audience. As the lights went down, I would turn slowly and regard the bodies in profile, with a deliberately neutral expression in my face. This, as I discovered through the run, was regarded variously as being sorrowful, triumphant, bewildered or empty – which shows how an audience will supply any ambiguity with an interpretation.

(McCabe, 210–11)

Antony Sher makes a similar observation about his Iago in Gregory Doran's 2004 RSC production but in this instance, although the director wanted ambiguity, it was the actor who was clear about the meaning of Iago's confrontational stare at the audience:

In our production, Iago was left in a sitting position after Othello wounded him; handcuffed, head bowed. Then after Lodovico's closing couplet, and just before a snap black out, we had Iago suddenly look up, confronting the audience with his eyes. Greg [the director] wanted the moment to be a strange, final aside, enigmatic, open to your own interpretation, but I was always clear about it myself. The dangerous wordsmith may be silent, but in my head this question always rang out: *You saw what was happening – why didn't you stop it?*

(Sher, 69)

Euphemism and Roderigo

If Iago speaks plainly to hint at (evasions of) larger narrative, he also uses the opposite tactic: euphemism. We cannot help but notice the number of occasions in this play in which communication is obfuscated because Iago uses a euphemism.

In 1.2 Cassio wonders why Othello is in the street outside the Sagittary. Iago explains metaphorically: 'Faith, he tonight hath boarded a land carrack: / If it prove lawful prize, he's made forever'. Cassio responds, not unreasonably, 'I do not understand'. Iago then offers the plain-English version: 'He's married' (1.2.49–52).

We see something similar in Act Four when Iago proposes 'the removing of Cassio'. Roderigo queries the euphemism: 'How do you mean, "removing" of him' (I have added the quotation marks here. Roderigo is clearly turning Iago's phrase back on him, querying the imprecision). Iago is forced to rephrase: 'Why, by making him uncapable of Othello's place'. This is still too indirect so he is obliged to continue bluntly: 'knocking out his brains' (4.2.229–30). Roderigo is still not won over, however, and the scene concludes with him requesting (and Iago guaranteeing) more justification:

> *Roderigo.* I will hear further reason for this.
> *Iago.*   And you shall be satisfied.
>
> (4.2.245)

This is characteristic of Roderigo's role in the play. Although Iago refers to him early on as 'this poor trash of Venice' (2.1.301) and later describes him, derogatively and dismissively, as 'a young quat [pimple]' that he 'has rubbed ... almost to the sense [to the quick]' (5.1. 11), to a large extent it is Roderigo who rubs Iago. Roderigo is the play's most persistent interrogator, holding Iago to account linguistically and logically, questioning both his vocabulary and his reasoning.

In the first scene, when Iago expounds his grievance against Othello (a long diatribe not just about his failure to be promoted but about Othello's promotion of a less experienced soldier), Roderigo objects logically, pragmatically, 'I would not follow him then'. This forces Iago to explain: 'I follow him to serve my turn upon him' (1.1.39–41).

In Act Four, Roderigo resists Iago's casting him as a gull. He is now suspicious and accuses Iago directly: 'I do not find that thou deal'st justly with me' (4.2.175). He accurately diagnoses Iago's *modus operandi* – 'your words and performances are no kin together' (4.2.184–5). This is the only time in the play that anyone confronts Iago with his tactics.

Roderigo's specific complaint is that he has seen no return on his investment: he has been sending jewels and gifts to Desdemona and she shows no sign of amorous gratitude to him. He tells Iago, 'the jewels you have had from me to deliver to Desdemona would half have corrupted a votarist [nun]' (4.2.188–90). Iago palms him off with generalizations – 'Well, go too; very well'. Roderigo protests at the reassurance, and at the vocabulary in which it is phrased, quoting it back at Iago: '"Very well", "go to"'! I cannot "go to", man, nor 'tis not "very well"'. (The first two sets of inverted commas are Honigmann's, the second two sets are mine – Roderigo is repeating the quotations.)

Roderigo here shows understanding of one of Iago's linguistic tactics, which is to utter generalities with authority. Normally we see this in the form of the aphorism: Iago utters aphoristic pronouncements as if they are proverbial wisdom. In fact they are (usually) statements that he is improvising. In Act Two when Roderigo complains about his cudgelling, Iago offers three aphorisms in four lines:

How poor are they that have not patience!
What wound did ever heal but by degrees?
Thou know'st we work by wit and not by witchcraft
And wit depends on dilatory time.

(2.3.365–8)

He continues: 'Though other things grow fair against the sun / Yet fruits that blossom first will first be ripe' (2.3.371–2). One editor paraphrases the second line as 'fruit trees that blossom first will produce ripe fruit first' and helpfully points out that 'this is not always true'; he further notes that in this 'false analogy blossom [is equated with] Cassio's cudgelling!' (Honigmann ed., 2.3.371–2n). The editor's exclamation mark

shows the preposterous nature of the analogy; but its prepos-
terousness is concealed by Iago's aphoristic phrasing which
gives an authority to statements and analogies that are far
from authoritative.

Iago pulls the wool over Othello's eyes (and over the eyes
of all those who describe him as 'honest' and 'kind': Montano,
Cassio, Desdemona). But Roderigo is not quite the gull he
is so easily dismissed as. Dramaturgically, he represents the
most effective (if ultimately ineffectual) opposition to Iago.
There are good reasons for this. Antony Sher recalls that in
the 2004 Royal Shakespeare Company production 'we sought
every opportunity to almost trip up Iago. Unless he's walking
a tightrope, everything becomes too easy' (Sher, 65). Roderigo
is, I think, an important part of the play's trip wires. Most
productions present him as a version of *Twelfth Night*'s Sir
Andrew Aguecheek, easily manipulatable, a lovesick fool who
talks of drowning. But in some productions, he is a consistent
thorn in Iago's flesh, showing up unexpectedly or not exiting
as planned, creating the potential for overhearing, forcing
Iago into reactive behaviour. The BBC film has an assertive
Roderigo, whose opening 'Tush, never tell me!' cuts Iago off,
forcing him into defensive explanation. And one of Roderigo's
thorn-in-the-flesh functions is to question Iago's language, as
no one else in the play does.

Proverbs

Othello contains a great number of proverbs. The Duke
speaks aphoristically in Act 1, scene 3 when he is trying to
reconcile Brabantio to the loss of his daughter:

> When remedies are past the griefs are ended
> By seeing the worst which late on hopes depended.
> To mourn a mischief that is past and gone
> Is the next way to draw new mischief on.

What cannot be preserved when fortune takes,
Patience her injury a mockery makes.
The robb'd that smiles steals something from the thief,
He robs himself that spends a bootless grief.

(1.3.203–10)

Brabantio sarcastically counters this consolation with

So let the Turk of Cyprus us beguile;
We lose it not, so long as we can smile.

(1.3.211–12)

The Duke's and Brabantio's lines about smiling while being robbed come back in Othello's lines in Act Three when, thinking about his previous ignorance of 'Cassio's kisses on her lips', he notes

He that is robbed, not wanting what is stolen,
Let him not know'it, and he's not robbed at all.

(3.3.345–6)

Proverbs constitute part of the play's recycling of language which we will examine in Chapter 3.

Proverbs are an interesting category of language. They embody received wisdom, common knowledge. They can thus be used as a particularly subtle form of persuasion. To say something in the form of a proverb is to say to the listener: 'we all know this and therefore you would be foolish to disagree'. It is notable how often Iago speaks in proverbs. But whereas the proverbs used by the other characters in the play can usually be found in one of the great collections of proverbs, R. W. Dent's *Shakespeare's Proverbial Language: An Index* (1981) or M. P. W. Tilley's *Dictionary of the Proverbs in England in the Sixteenth and Seventeenth Centuries* (1950), Iago's proverbs are often improvisatory; his language is only made to sound proverbial. He invents proverbs, giving his language the status of truth, preventing questioning. When the *New York Times* theatre critic reviewed Simon Russell Beale's performance as Iago in 1998, he noted that Iago's phrase to Roderigo, 'Put money in thy purse', was repeated by Beale 'like a folksy, *adage-sprouting* uncle' (Brantley, my italics). Indeed – sprouting adages is one of Iago's linguistic tactics.

When Roderigo complains about the lack of results in Act Two, Iago consoles him, Duke-like, with the series of proverbial aphorisms quoted in full at the end of the previous section ('How poor are they that have not patience! ...'; 2.3.365–8). Iago here appropriates the Duke's role as authority figure, offering authoritative wisdom in the linguistically packaged form of the proverb. He had done the same in an earlier conversation with Roderigo, telling him that 'the wine she [Desdemona] drinks is made of grapes' (2.1.249–50); Honigmann comments that this is 'one of Iago's vague general assertions, which we have to interpret for ourselves' (Honigmann ed., 2.1.249–50n). And when Iago concludes a soliloquy with 'Knavery's plain [honest] face is never seen till used' (2.1.310), he provides an indirect justification for his tactics by his covert appeal to proverbial precedent.

Separate languages

Characters in plays, like characters in life, have idiolects – individual ways of speaking that identify them. *Othello* uses idiolects to create different narrative ambiences, some of which come into conflict within a single conversation or scene. Iago's conversation, for instance, is pruriently and reductively sexual. The result is that he seems to be speaking a different language from the other characters; indeed, they frequently do not understand him. We see this in the play's opening scene.

Iago calls to Brabantio that 'an old black ram / Is tupping your white ewe' (1.1.87–8). Brabantio's incredulous reaction

– 'Have you lost your wits?' (1.1.91) – could be prompted either by the content of Iago's speech or by its coarseness. Iago's next lines continue the animal metaphor: 'you'll have your daughter covered with a Barbary horse; you'll have your nephews [descendants] neigh to you, you'll have coursers [horses] for cousins and jennets [small horses] for germans [relatives]' (1.1.109–12). Brabantio's reply makes specific his earlier reaction about Iago's loss of wits, calling Iago a 'profane wretch' (1.1.113): only someone out of his mind could utter such obscenities. Undaunted, Iago continues in the same bestial vein: 'your daughter and the Moor are now making the beast with two backs' (1.1.114–15). Roderigo takes over the narrative and, in contrast, offers a clear summary: 'your fair daughter /… [is] transported with no worse nor better guard / But with a knave of common hire, a gondolier, / To the gross clasps of a lascivious Moor' (1.1.120–4). Whereas Roderigo's speech provides information, Iago's speech is not communicative; it is phatic. (Phatic speech creates atmosphere rather than communicating ideas.) This is true of Iago's speech throughout.

The linguistic disjunction of the opening scene is replayed in 1.2 when Cassio enters. Cassio asks Iago why Othello is in the street outside the Sagittary. Iago replies with a physically salacious metaphor: 'Faith, he hath tonight boarded a land carrack: / If it prove lawful prize, he's made forever' (1.2.50–1). Cassio's response is a perfectly reasonable incomprehension – 'I do not understand' – thereby forcing Iago to provide the clarity he had previously eschewed: 'He's married' (1.2.52).

We hear the same disjunction at the end of the play when Iago broaches murder to Roderigo: 'the removing of Cassio' (4.2.229). Roderigo is cautious, requesting linguistic precision: 'How do you mean, "removing" of him?' (I have added the inverted commas to highlight Roderigo's quoting of Iago's euphemism.) (4.2.230). Iago remains imprecise ('Why, by making him incapable of Othello's place') before yielding to Roderigo's continued hesitance or incomprehension with the explanatory 'knocking out his brains' (4.2.230–2).

A similar disjunction of language (and hence of tone) is clear in Act Two in the two conversations Iago has about Desdemona, the first with Roderigo, the second with Cassio. In 2.1, Roderigo uses the language of divinity to summarize Desdemona: 'she's full of most blest condition' (2.1.247–8). Iago dismisses this with a contemptuous exclamation ('Blest fig's-end!') and an equalizing observation: 'The wine she drinks is made of grapes' (2.1.249–50). (His oenological image simply means 'she's no better than the rest of us'.)

We hear an action replay of this contrast between divinity and reduction in Act 2, scene 3. Cassio speaks a Petrarchan language of devotion which Iago tries to redirect towards sexual smuttiness. (The love lyrics of the Italian poet Francesco Petrarca (1304–74) put the beloved on a pedestal and approached her as an object of worship. Petrarch's name provides us with the adjective for this kind of love poem.)

It is worth spending some time on this scene. Cassio is professionally vigilant and says 'we must to the watch' (2.3.12). Iago says it's too early and the only reason they have been dismissed is because Othello wants to go to bed with his bride: 'he hath not yet made wanton the night with her, and she is sport for Jove' (2.3.16–17). Here he introduces a sexually salacious evaluation, saying that a ladies' man like Jove would find Desdemona an attractive sexual option.

Cassio closes down the lewdness, redefining the terms of the dialogue:

Cassio.	She's a most exquisite lady.
Iago.	And I'll warrant her full of game.
Cassio.	Indeed she's a most fresh and delicate creature.
Iago.	What an eye she has! methinks it sounds a parley to provocation.
Cassio.	An inviting eye; and yet methinks right modest.
Iago.	And when she speaks is it not an alarum to love?
Cassio.	She is indeed perfection.

(2.3.18–25)

You can see the contrasting attitudes in the dialogue; they contrast in both attitude and language (the former determines the latter). Cassio introduces class ('lady'). A lady is not a sexual plaything (this one word, 'lady', rebuts Iago's 'sport for Jove') or an object. Instead Cassio evaluates Desdemona in terms that are socially and poetically sanctioned: she is 'exquisite'. This is an aesthetically evaluative adjective that he will use again in this scene: 'this is a more exquisite song than the other' (2.394–5). In this one sentence Cassio counters and tries to redirect Iago's previous remark.

Iago refuses to be deflected. Desdemona, he says, is 'full of game'; her eye is 'a parley to provocation' (2.3.18, 21–2). Once again he is defining Desdemona sexually, in the same way as Ulysses does Cressida in *Troilus and Cressida* when he says, 'There's language in her eye, her cheek, her lip, / Nay, her foot speaks' (4.5.56–7). Iago says the same thing. 'Parley' (from French *parler*) is a verbal invitation; Desdemona has a 'come hither' look.

Cassio politely agrees that Desdemona has 'an inviting eye' but he corrects the sexual direction of the conversation: 'and yet me thinks *right modest*' (my italics). You can hear his continued determination to rescue the conversation (and Desdemona's reputation). Iago is not so easily diverted: 'And when she speaks is it not an alarum to love' [i.e. is not her voice a turn-on?]. Cassio offers a general summary that is far from sexual: 'She is indeed perfection' (2.3.25). This is the territory of Petrarchan worship. It is also a rephrasing of his statement at line 18: 'She's a most exquisite lady'. Cassio has not budged an inch in this dialogue. Iago realizes he is getting nowhere so he closes down the conversation: 'Well: happiness to their sheets!' (2.3.18–26).

We hear two languages here in the two sides of the dialogue: the language of physical lust and the language of Petrarchan adoration. Trevor Nunn's 1989 RSC production with its barracks setting gave this dialogue a locker-room boys'-talk quality. (Or, at least, as we have just seen, Iago was trying to create such an atmosphere but Cassio resisted all such linguistic overtures.) The RSC production in 1999, directed by Michael Attenborough, played this conversation as 'an attempt to get Cassio to admit to sexual awareness of her [Desdemona]. This could then be used against him to Othello, as evidence of his lust for her' (McCabe, 198). But the attempt fails. The actor Richard McCabe writes that his Iago had this dialogue in mind in his later 'highlighting of their markedly differing qualities' (McCabe, 198):

> He hath a daily beauty in his life
> That makes me ugly.

(5.1.19–20)

That difference is expressed in language.

We have already heard Cassio speak this Petrarchan language – a language unintelligible to Montano when in 2.1 they were waiting at the quayside. Cassio describes the general's wife in hyperbolic terms:

> he hath achieved a maid
> That paragons descriptions and wild fame;
> One that exceeds the quirks of blazoning pens
> And in th'essential vesture of creation
> Does tire the inginir.

(2.1.61–5)

(A rough paraphrase: Desdemona surpasses all description, even the wildest; she outdoes the description of the most gifted poet; her essential beauty even exhausts the creator.) As you can see from the inadequacy of my paraphrase, the language is complex and it is no surprise that for the last line the Quarto text substitutes the simpler 'does bear all excellence' (McMillin ed., 2.1.70,).

When news comes of the arrival of Iago's ship, Cassio becomes rhapsodic:

> Tempests themselves, high seas, and howling winds, ...
> As having sense of beauty, do omit
> Their mortal natures, letting go safely by
> The divine Desdemona.

$$(2.1.68–73)$$

He is still speaking to Montano, the Governor of Cyprus, who does not connect this language of divinity with their immediately preceding conversation regarding Othello's wife and has to ask 'What is she?'. Cassio explains, 'she that I spake of', and then kneels in adoration as Desdemona disembarks:

> The riches of the ship is come ashore:
> You men of Cyprus, let her have your knees!
> Hail to thee, lady, and the grace of heaven,
> Before, behind thee, and on every hand
> Enwheel thee round!

$$(2.1.83–7)$$

One can see why Verdi's opera (*Otello*, 1887) provides an *Ave Maria* in its score: the music in the last Act, when Desdemona prays, expresses something that is already in Shakespeare's language here.

Characters in plays usually have different linguistic patterns (stage character is created by rhetorical recognition: we know who characters are because of how they speak; see Melchiori) but in *Othello* the idiolects almost amount to different languages – languages that are not readily recognized or understood by others on stage. When Othello accuses Desdemona in the bedchamber in Act Four she says:

> What doth your speech import?
> I understand a fury in your words
> But not the words.

$$(4.2.31–3)$$

In a scene of linguistic misunderstanding between a lord and a charlatan in *All's Well that Ends Well*, the lord asks in bewilderment 'Is't not a language I speak?' (2.3.189). His question could apply to *Othello* in its entirety: this is a play in which characters do not understand each other's language.

Reception

From here it is easy to see how miscommunication arises. Part of the play's pain (for us) comes from the characters' unawareness of the meaning their words or lines or behaviours have for others. For Desdemona, insistent questions regarding Cassio's reinstatement represent connubial intimacy, for Othello marital infidelity. Desdemona's moist hand is to her a sign of her carefree youth, to Othello it is evidence of a licentious nature. Iago reinterprets Cassio's quayside 'courtesy' as 'lechery' (2.1.254–5). The Cassio who came 'a-wooing' can be both a companion and a rival (the form of the word, with its 'a-' prefix, means both). When Othello refers to his forehead, to Desdemona this means he has a headache, to Othello that he is a cuckold. Iago later exploits this divergence of meaning. He asks if Othello has hurt his head during his epileptic fit, a question that pains Othello because of its associations:

Iago.	How is it, general? have you not hurt your head?
Othello.	Dost thou mock me?
Iago.	I mock you? no, by heaven! Would you would bear your fortune like a man!
Othello.	A horned man's a monster and a beast.

(4.1.58–62)

We have earlier seen an identical sequence after the brawl with Iago's apparently solicitous question to the wounded Cassio:

Iago.	What, are you hurt, lieutenant?
Cassio.	Ay, past all surgery.
Iago.	Marry, God forbid!
Cassio.	Reputation, reputation, reputation!

(2.3.255–8)

And when Cassio laments the side effects of alcohol ('that men should put an enemy in their mouths, to steal away their brains'; 2.3.286–7) or Othello laments the 'curse of marriage' – 'That we can call these delicate creatures ours / And not their appetites' (3.3.272–4) – I am struck by the way these phrases can describe language in this play, and language in general: there is a mismatch between mouth and mind, we do not own the meaning of what we say (see Gross, 819).

Literary texts are akin to performances in which an author's intended meaning is not passively transmitted but created in the process of reception by reader or audience (Hawthorn, 107). Meaning is not monolithic but constructed anew (or differently) at the moment of reception. This was the theme of a 1992 play by David Mamet, *Oleanna*, in which a university professor who teaches about the transactional nature of communication fails to apply it in his own life:

Carol.	A *joke* you have told, with a sexist tinge. The language you use, a verbal or physical caress, yes, yes, I know, you say that it is meaningless. I understand. I differ from you. To lay a hand on someone's shoulder.
John.	It was devoid of sexual content.
Carol.	I say it was not. I SAY IT WAS NOT. Don't you begin to *see* ... ? Don't you *begin to understand*? IT'S NOT FOR YOU TO SAY.

(Mamet, 70)

If meaning is transactional and mobile, the handkerchief in *Othello* starts to function as a symbol of language – it is detachable, gets passed around, accrues (different) meanings. It goes from its source to Othello's mother (or father), to Othello to Desdemona to the floor to Emilia to Iago to the window ledge in Cassio's chamber to Cassio to Bianca. And at each stage it 'means' differently: Bianca sees it as evidence that Cassio has found a 'newer friend' (3.4.181), Emilia as a means of regaining her husband's affection, Othello as proof of disloyalty. And just as Othello reads the handkerchief as 'honour', so we (mis)read language as fixed in meaning. But anything that is detachable is capable of misinterpretation (cf. Stallybrass, 137–8).

The handkerchief – a textile – is associated with language in another way. The word 'text' comes from the Latin noun *textus*, meaning 'something woven'. We cannot help but notice the association of textile and textual terms in this play – for example, Iago complains that Othello evades the intercessories who plead for him with 'a *bombast* circumstance / Horribly *stuffed* with epithets of war' (1.1.12–13, my italics). ('Bombast' is cotton or cotton wool, used for 'stuffing' clothes.) We are only a few lines into the play but already the rhetorical and the textile are linked. The later significance of the handkerchief in a play about language and meaning should come as no surprise.

Speak 'parrot?' (2.3.275)

One of the problems with language in *Othello* is the curious way in which speeches come back in different contexts, forming echoes and verbal matrices. In the Senate scene Brabantio's parting shot to Othello is:

> Look to her, Moor, if thou hast eyes to see:
> She has deceived her father, and may thee.

> (1.3.293–4)

Arguably, the seeds of Othello's suspicion are sown in these lines by Brabantio. The phrase reappears manipulatively in Iago's dialogue with Othello:

Iago.   She did deceive her father, marrying you, ...
Othello.   And so she did.
Iago.   Why, go to then:
                 She that so young could give out such a
                 seeming
                 To seel her father's eyes up, close as oak –
                                                   (3.3.209–13)

From here, the play uncouples phrases and their referents.
If you encountered the following phrases out of dramatic
context, would you know who is being described?

1

   a slipper and subtle knave, a finder out of occasions, that
   has an eye, can stamp and counterfeit advantages, though
   true advantage never present itself – a devilish knave.
                                                   (2.1.239–2)

It sounds like a perfect description of Iago (it *is* a perfect
description of Iago). But in fact, it is Iago's description of
Cassio.

2

Who says they 'beguile the thing I am by seeming otherwise'
(2.1.122–3). Iago? This is indeed what he does – but this
phrase describes, and is spoken by, Desdemona.

3

Who is the jealous husband who describes his pain as
follows? –

   The thought whereof [of being cuckolded]
   Doth like a poisonous mineral gnaw my inwards ...

                                                   (2.1.294–5)

This jealous husband is not Othello but Iago.

4

Iago.   Work on,
               My medicine, work! Thus credulous fools are
               caught,
               And many worthy and chaste dames even thus,
               All guiltless, meet reproach – What ho! my
               lord!
               My lord, I say! Othello!

                                        (4.1.44–7)

Technically, the 'many worthy and chaste dames' who 'meet reproach' must refer to Desdemona. But David Suchet reads this line as referring to Othello (Suchet, 195). This is a defensible reading or misreading – partly because of Iago's trademark 'and' (we will explore this in Chapter 3) which can equate two equal components (Othello is a credulous fool, *like* a trapped guiltless dame) or can develop a sequence (Othello is a credulous fool; *furthermore*, Desdemona is not the first chaste dame to meet reproach).

5

               A sibyl that had numbered in the world
               The sun to course two hundred compasses
               In her prophetic fury sewed the work [the handkerchief].

                                        (3.4.72–4)

Does this means that the sibyl was 200 years old (a sybil whose years were equal in number to 200 compasses of the sun)? (Many critics read the line this way.) Or that she prophesied that the earth had 200 years to go (a sybil who had calculated that the sun still had 200 compasses of the earth to make)? The line probably has the latter meaning but you can see why one might be tempted by the former.

6

In Act Two we encounter two phrases that are near-identical. When Cassio describes Desdemona to Montano as 'our great captain's captain' (2.1.74) he foreshadows a sentiment that Iago will express two scenes later when Iago tells the cashiered lieutenant that 'our general's wife is now the general' (2.3.309–10). However, the metaphors and paradoxes are not as synonymous as they sound: this expression of a positive, marital inseparation, the two-in-one of marriage, is confused by language because the first of these phrases is a compliment; the other, spoken by Iago, is pejorative. Out of context would we know which is which?

Something similar happens in Act Four when Emilia, in her first astonished reaction to the evidence of Othello's jealousy and suspicion about the handkerchief, rages against 'some eternal villain / Some busy and insinuating rogue, / Some cogging, cozening slave' who has 'devised this slander' to 'get some office' (4.2.132–5). She has hit the hail on the head: this is not just an accurate description of her husband but an accurate description of the plot. However, she is oblivious to the applicability of her words. (But not always: in some productions this is a lightbulb moment. However, some productions offer the opposite interpretation: an Emilia who is determined to believe the best of her husband. In Act Five Emilia urges Iago to clear his reputation – 'I know thou did'st not [tell Othello that Desdemona was unfaithful], thou'rt not such a villain' (5.2.170). In the BBC film, Emilia desperately emphasized *know*, willing her husband to be the character she believes him to be. In the Johannesburg Market Theatre production the emphasis was on *such* – here what was at stake was not Iago's villainy, already known to his wife, but its extent.)

Language gets recycled in another way when a character's speech ends up in another's mouth. The play begins with Iago quoting Othello: 'For "Certes", says he, / "I have already chose my officer" (1.1.15–16). He later speaks for Cassio

(Cassio is mute: 'I cannot speak'; 2.3.185) and, later still, quotes Cassio, talking in his sleep.

These flexible phrases show that it is not Desdemona who is promiscuous but language. And when Cassio expresses horror at the effects of his inebriation – 'drunk? and speak parrot?' (2.3.275) – he inadvertently describes one effect of language: used thoughtlessly, it has the potential to turn us into parrots.

Speaking 'stoutly' (3.1.45)

After the brawl on the first night in Cyprus, Cassio wastes no time in planning his campaign for reinstatement: he immediately sends for Emilia to ask her to procure him access to Desdemona (3.1.34–6). Emilia's reassurance to Cassio in Act Three is lengthy and conclusive. She tells him that Desdemona is doing everything she can and that Othello has already promised to reinstate Cassio as soon as it is compatible with diplomatic relations with Cyprus. That should end the conversation. Cassio unnecessarily continues – and the unnecessary nature of his response is indicated by the opening adverb, 'yet':

> *Yet* I beseech you, …
> Give me advantage of some brief discourse
> With Desdemon alone.

> (3.1.52–5; my emphasis)

The opportunity ('advantage') Cassio requests here arises almost immediately, in a scene which smacks of conclusion from its start:

> Be thou assured, good Cassio, I will do
> All my abilities in thy behalf.

> (3.3.1–2)

This sounds like a reassuring dismissal of Cassio. But the dialogue is extended by Emilia's reinforcement ('Good madam, do'; 3–4) and Cassio's effusive compliment:

> Bounteous madam,
> Whatever shall become of Michael Cassio,
> He's never anything but your true servant.

> (3.3.7–10)

This prompts Desdemona's further terminative reassurance ('be you well assured / He shall in strangeness stand no farther off / Than in a politic distance'; 11–13), only to be met with Cassio's introduction of possible difficulties.

As in 3.1, when Cassio prolonged the conversation by introducing an unnecessary extension with 'yet', here his use of 'but' introduces the possible difficulties. He picks up Desdemona's assurance that his estrangement is short-term for diplomatic reasons ('politic') and wonders what will happen if that 'policy' negligently becomes long-term:

> Ay, but lady,
> That policy may either last so long,
> Or feed upon such nice and waterish diet,
> Or breed itself so out of circumstance,
> That I, being absent and my place supplied,
> My general will forget my love and service.

> (3.3.13–18)

Desdemona responds by repeating what she had said 14 lines earlier: 'Do not doubt'. In the BBC film Penelope Wilton's Desdemona was tolerant but frustrated; despite her politeness she was, at least initially, trying to get rid of Cassio – 'Do not doubt' (3.3.5–7), 'Be you well assured' (3.3.11–13), 'Do not doubt that' (3.3.19). One can even see how a case could be made here for Iago's earlier description of Cassio as a 'subtle knave, a finder out of occasions, that has an eye, can stamp and counterfeit advantages, though true advantage never present itself' (2.1.239–2); it would be easy to play a narcissistic Cassio in this scene, thinking only of himself.

What Cassio wants is speech; and consequently Emilia promises to 'bestow [him] where [he] shall have time / To speak [his] bosom freely' (3.1.57). 'Bestow' is a neutral verb – it simply means 'to place' – but it is often used in illicit situations. Polonius and Claudius 'bestow' themselves to eavesdrop on Ophelia and Hamlet (*Hamlet* 3.1.33, 44). When a gentleman asks a lady's waiting-woman to conceal him somewhere for private conference with another man's wife, it is a generically problematic request. It moves us into the world of cuckold comedy or political treachery even before Iago draws attention to the meeting with his 'Ha, I like not that' (3.3.34).

Desdemona is confident of her linguistic effect on Othello – 'I'll … talk him out of patience' she says (3.3.23) – an effect she invites Cassio to witness as an audience member: 'stay and hear me speak' (3.3.31). It is Cassio's refusal to be an audience that gives Iago his first opportunity to insinuate: 'Ha, I like not that … I cannot think it / That he [Cassio] would steal away so guilty-like' (3.3.34, 38–9). And given that the play stages the competition for authority in terms of who commands audience or is an attentive auditor, Cassio in a sense digs his own grave: he declines opportunities both to speak and to listen. After the debacle on the watch he says, 'I cannot speak', allowing Iago to speak (misleadingly) on his behalf (2.3.185). At the end of that scene Iago invites Cassio to 'sue to' Othello (2.3.271); Cassio declines ('I will rather sue to be despised'; 2.3.273). When Iago persists, Cassio simply takes both sides of the dialogue as read, supplying Othello's response: 'I will ask him for my place again, he shall tell me I am a drunkard' (2.3.298–9). And now here at the start of 3.3 he declines to be an audience to Desdemona's speech. Cassio speaks 'stoutly' – to the wrong person. He refuses to speak to the right person or even to be in his company when someone else speaks for him. Acts of narration are bound up with auditors and audience – one needs to know when and to whom to direct one's speech.

Audience

Narrative requires an audience (or, as Othello puts it, 'a greedy ear'; 1.3.150). *Othello* is very audience-aware, as we shall see in Chapter 3 when we consider language and the theatre. At the moment I am concerned not so much with theatre audience as with audition *per se* and the ways in which speakers in *Othello* command or need others' attention. In 1976 Marjorie Pryse identified this need as a characteristic of the play: the characters compete for auditors and audience and Othello's insecurities emerge when he realizes that he no longer has Desdemona as his sole audience – that she listens to Cassio, for example.

This rhetorical observation is bound up with identity. If speech most shows a man (as Shakespeare's contemporary, the poet and playwright Ben Jonson, said, quoting the ancients), then we have identity only in as much as there is someone to listen to us. In a sense, this observation cannot be separated from the theatrical tropes in the play that I have deferred to Chapter 3. Tom Stoppard's Player in his play *Rosencrantz and Guildenstern are Dead* talks of 'the single assumption which makes our existence viable – that somebody is watching' (Stoppard, 63). For 'watching' we could substitute (or *to* 'watching' we could *add*) 'listening'. Actors need audiences; speakers need audiences. The common denominator is audition.

Othello begins with a failure to listen. Iago has employed three 'great ones of the city, / In personal suit to make me his lieutenant' (1.1.7–8). These go-betweens find that their plea falls on deaf ears; Othello 'nonsuits my mediators' – he 'stops the suit of, refuses' (Honigmann's gloss; the verb is unique in Shakespeare). By Act Three, the balance of power has changed: Othello has ears only for Iago. And Iago uses the same witchcraft that Othello has used: language (Pryse, 469).

Throughout the play we see petitions to listen, protests about those who do not listen, and invitations to stay on stage and audit. Iago's first line in the play is a frustrated protest that Roderigo is not listening properly, "Sblood, but you'll not hear me' (1.1.4). Othello loves Desdemona because she is such a good audience: 'This to hear / Would Desdemona seriously incline' (1.3.146–7). Desdemona herself encourages Othello to associate audition with love: 'if I had a friend that loved her, / I should but teach him how to tell my story / And that would woo her' (1.3.165–7). On the quayside she offers herself as audience to Iago and although she tells us that she is an unwilling audience (2.1.122–3), she extends the encounter by asking Iago, 'Come, how wouldst thou praise me?' (2.1.124). After the brawl on the watch, the cashiered Cassio anticipates Othello's audience reaction (as we saw in the previous section), giving us a play-within-a-play: 'I will ask him for my place again, he shall tell me I am a drunkard' (2.3.298–9). After Cassio is cashiered, Desdemona listens to the lieutenant and speaks for him: Emilia reassures Cassio, 'The general and his wife are talking of it, / And she speaks for you stoutly' (3.1.44–50). Desdemona has confidence in her power to turn Othello into audience when she promises Cassio's reinstatement: 'I'll intermingle everything he does with Cassio's suit' (3.3.25–6). When she speaks on Cassio's behalf, as we saw above, Cassio declines to be an audience (3.3.31–2). The list-like quality of this paragraph shows the way the play stresses acts of speaking and listening.

In the teasing dialogue with Othello that follows Cassio's exit, Desdemona lets slip two potentially wounding pieces of information – that she views her husband as 'mamm'ring' and that she has spoken 'dispraisingly' of him to Cassio (3.3.70, 72).

Whether 'mamm'ring' means 'hesitating' or 'stammering', Honigmann notes that it is 'an unkind word' (3.3.70n). For a hero whose marital identity is constructed as rhetorician and narrator, this dispraise is a challenge to his self-presentation as Desdemona's romantic hero (Pryse, 467). It is this power of rhetoric that Othello tries to recuperate in Act Five when he delays his death with an inset narrative.

Desdemona's idle musings on Lodovico in 4.3 focus on the nobleman's rhetorical ability – 'he speaks well' (4.3.36). Emilia's affirmative but apparently illogical response – 'I know a lady in Venice would have walked barefoot to Palestine for a touch of his nether lip (4.3.37–8) – shows the play's equation of linguistic with sexual power.

Desdemona's line is controversial. The conversation is not in the Quarto text, which, as we saw in the Introduction, shortens the dialogue between Desdemona and Emilia considerably and omits the willow song. (The dialogue you will find in Honigmann's edition at 4.3.29–52 is a Folio-only dialogue.) The Folio presents the sequence as follows, where it is Desdemona who first turns the conversation to Lodovico:

Des.	This *Lodouico* is a proper man.
Æmel.	A very handsome man.
Des.	He speakes well.
Æmi.	I know a Lady in Venice would haue walk'd barefoot to Palestine for a touch of his nether lip.

(sig. vv3r, TLN 3006–10)

Many editions reassign the line about Lodovico to Emilia, and Honigmann explains why: 'for Desdemona to praise Lodovico at this point seems out of character' (4.3.34–5n). But it is not out of character for the *play*, which associates rhetorical ability with a listener's approval. And in the Folio version of the dialogue we see/hear a replay of what happened earlier in the 'locker room' dialogue between Iago and Cassio: two characters speaking different languages. Desdemona speaks of accomplishments: Lodovico is perfect ('proper') and articulate ('he speakes well'). Emilia thinks of physicality – good looks ('A very handsome man') and kissability ('a touch of his nether lip').

This is a world in which story-telling matters: you can win (or lose) a professional position (Iago, Cassio), a bride (Othello) or your life (Desdemona), depending on how you command an audience or to whom you give an audience. Othello's sexual suspicion becomes more understandable: Desdemona's audition of him led to love; he sees her grant audience to Cassio and therefore ... Furthermore, since misogynist metonymy (*metonymy* is the substitution of one thing for another) associated the open mouth with the open vagina (the logic was that a woman who opens one orifice – her mouth – will open another), an early modern husband had material to fuel his jealousy.

When Shakespeare restages Othello's jealousy in King Leontes in *The Winter's Tale*, he replays this association between a wife's power to command an audience and a husband's consequent insecurity. Leontes' wife, Hermione, is initially silent ('Tongue-tied, our queen?'; 1.2.27). Leontes asks her to persuade the visiting Polixenes to extend his stay. Hermione obeys and is successful in her task. Leontes is immediately suspicious ('At my request he would not'; 1.2.87), a suspicion prompted by the perceived diminution of his rhetorical ability. He conflates Hermione's rhetorical efficacy with her erotic power (Enterline, 198–9). This association is unwittingly furthered by Hermione herself when she summarizes her life's two rhetorical achievements:

> I have spoken to the purpose twice;
> The one, for ever earn'd a royal husband;
> Th'other, for some while a friend.

(1.2.106–8)

Leontes misreads the equal syntactical weight as equal sexual attraction.

But audience does not just mean auditor. It has a theatrical valence too. As Iago gains narrative power, he moves from story-telling to staging. Iago's role is full of implied stage directions, such as when he concludes that Emilia must speak to Cassio on Desdemona's behalf: 'I'll set her on' (2.3.378–9). He not only narrates Cassio's dream, he performs it. (At least, this is how many modern productions stage the narrative.) He not only invents a narrative of the handkerchief, he stage-manages it: 'I will in Cassio's lodging lose this napkin / And let him find it' (3.3.324–5). He stages a pantomime of overseeing/overhearing when he places Othello at the edge of the stage in 4.1. Thus Iago not only stage-manages props (the handkerchief), he stage-manages bodies as props. Auditors and actors start to merge; actors and audience start to merge. Iago, that Janus-figure, the guardian of the threshold, blurs boundaries on stage as he does in language.

Words and deeds

It is notable how often the play cues our expectation of something dramatic, only to divert it into language. In the opening scene, Iago tries to 'stage manage a scuffle' (Jones 1971, 129) but his instigations to violence lead only to Othello's dignified refusal to fight – 'keep up your bright swords, for the dew will rust them' (1.2.59). This is the pattern of the first two acts of *Othello*: we have 'a desire for something to happen, at times even an appetite for violence – but an appetite which is so far frustrated' (Jones 1971, 134). In the Senate scene for instance, we get story-telling, not the trial scene of *The Merchant of Venice*: Othello 'for a second time refuses to "make a scene": that is to say he refuses to exhibit passion' (Jones 1971, 129).

When Iago gains control of the play, his stage-management increases the tempo, introduces farce, and leads Othello to make a scene in the most savage and violent way. Othello regains narrative control only at the last minute. The implied 'exeunt' at 5.2.335 (Lodovico has dispatched Othello and Iago, concluding 'Come, bring him away') is interrupted by Othello asking to speak a 'word or two'; language and narrative extend the play. His last speech, which is indirectly his last address to the Senate (since he is directing Lodovico as to what to report), is exactly the same length – eighteen and a half lines – as his first address to the Senate (Jones 1971, 148). And it has the same rhetorical structure of anaphora (repetition of a word in successive clauses or lines). The preposition 'of' cues the order in both: '*Of* moving accidents … / *Of* hair-breadth scapes … / *Of* being taken … *of* my redemption' in the Senate speech (1.3.136–9, my italics); '*Of* one that loved not wisely … / *Of* one not easily jealous … / *of* whose hand … / *of* one whose subdued eyes' in the suicide speech (5.2.342–6, my italics).

It is worth looking at this speech – or its implications in the play – because 'speak of me as I am' is no longer as straightforward an instruction as it might have been – or as it is at the end of other Shakespeare plays. Iago does not request that we speak of him as he is – unsurprisingly, given that he is not what he is. But Othello's identity may be similarly unstable; we may never have seen or known Othello's self. His autobiographical account of wooing Desdemona is a narrative account of himself (one which, as we saw above, does not tally with Desdemona's account), and since his concluding tale results in suicide ('I took by th'throat the circumcised dog / And smote him thus'; 5.2.353–4), blending the teller of the tale and its protagonist, we may be no further forward. As killer and killed, Othello has a narrative duality.

Before we look at the duality in Othello's final speech, let us consider the duality of words.

Words and things

Iago's tactic is to hold words up to Othello who then has a visual image of an action. Words create reality; consequently, 'the plot of *Othello* ... derives from an act that never occurred' (Wilder, 140).

Sixteenth-century intellectuals were very interested in the relation between words and things, between the word and the named environment. The text on which debate focused was Adam's naming of the animals in Genesis 2.19: 'and whatsoever Adam called every living creature, that was the name thereof'. To us today, these early chapters of Genesis seem straightforward; to the early modern mind they were very difficult to interpret. This line illustrates why. Adam's naming of the animals permits two, opposed, interpretations. In one interpretation, Adam assigned names arbitrarily, and it is convention – the way we agree to use words – which gives them their 'meaning'. Shakespeare's Juliet is a proponent of this theory: 'a rose / By any other word would smell as sweet' (2.2.43–4). An alternative view is that Adam gave the animals the names that suited their personality and thus language simply provides labels for a pre-existing identity. This line in Genesis was key to early modern theories of language and identity, name and thing.

In the Introduction we looked at the several ways in which *Othello* examines the relation between name and thing, and the ways Iago systematically destroys the link between name and identity, between personal name and positional name. In Act Four Desdemona too examines the fissure Iago has created:

Desdemona. Am I that name, Iago?
Iago. What name, fair lady?
Desdemona. Such as she said my lord did say I was.

(4.2.119–21)

In the world of *Othello* confidence in reference is ruptured: 'Men should be what they seem' (3.3.129) becomes 'I think my wife be honest, and think she is not' (3.3.387). The play ends not with Othello but with 'he that was Othello' (5.2.281). Personal name, personal identity; professional name, professional identity: lose one part of the symbiosis and you lose the other.

And so we come back to our investigation into what it means to 'speak of me as I am'. We may begin our inquiry by looking at other plays – other Shakespeare tragedies – in which the hero is summarized in narrative.

Narrating the hero

Mark Antony tells us that Brutus was 'the noblest Roman of them all: / All the conspirators, save only he, / Did that they did in envy of great Caesar'. He offers the soundbite summary: 'This was a man!' (*Julius Caesar* 5.5.69–71, 76). In *Coriolanus* Aufidius commands the drum to 'speak mournfully' and pikes to be trailed in deference, and he promises that Coriolanus 'shall have a noble memory' (5.6.149, 153). Fortinbras says that Hamlet 'was likely, had he been put on [become king], / To have prov'd most royal' (5.2.402–3). Hamlet, in a variant of Othello, asks his friend Horatio to 'report me and my cause aright / To the unsatisfied' (5.2.344–5) and Horatio offers a trailer of the story he will tell: 'So shall you hear / Of carnal, bloody, and unnatural acts, / Of accidental judgments, casual slaughters, / Of deaths put on by cunning and forc'd cause, / And, in this upshot, purposes mistook / Fall'n on the inventors' heads'. The characters exeunt to form this audience: 'Let us haste to hear it' (*Hamlet* 5.2.385–91). So too at the end of *Romeo and Juliet*: 'Go hence to have more talk of these sad things ... / For never was a story of more woe / Than this of Juliet and her Romeo' (5.3.306, 308–9).

In Shakespearean comedy, narrative is not a problem. Comedy has the leisure to include narrative; it has no need to gesture towards it in an unwritten Act Six, after the death of the hero. Autobiographical monologue is invited at the opening of *Comedy of Errors*, and the play has time to indulge the narrative when the arrested Egeon tells his story of disasters. Even in its most abbreviated form, as at the end of *Pericles* where the story of Marina's life is reduced to three nouns (a tempest, a birth, a death; 5.3.33–4), language in comedy is never problematic:

> Is it no more to be your daughter
> Than to say my mother's name was Thaisa?

> (*Pericles* 5.1.198–9)

But in tragedy language is dangerous. To Cordelia in the opening scene of *King Lear*, 'nothing' is a declaration of honesty, to her father, Lear, it is an instance of filial ingratitude. In *Hamlet* stable family relationships collapse logistically (Gertrude's remarriage to her brother-in-law makes her an 'aunt-mother' and him an 'uncle-father'; 2.2.372) just as in *Romeo and Juliet* 'my only hate' becomes 'my only love' (1.5.137), enemy becomes husband and foe becomes wife. For Desdemona, as we saw above, persistence about Cassio's reinstatement signals a desire to help; for Othello it indicates lechery.

In requesting that the onstage assembly 'speak of [him] as [he is]', Othello reverts to a successful tactic from the beginning of the play. Accused of stealing Desdemona by witchcraft, he summoned Desdemona: '*Let her speak of me* before her father' (1.3.117; my italics). In that instance, he was exculpated. He hopes the same will apply in Act Five.

But there is a difference. The conclusion asks the Venetians to speak of Othello 'as I am'; 'as I am' is the very concept that has been put under pressure (in language and in practice) throughout the play. Othello has been called a barbarian – one who babbles, from the Greek *barbaros* – an identity he belies in his commanding oratory, yet occupies in Desdemona's tease ('mamm'ring on') and is made to occupy in Iago's machinations which result not just in psychological but in syntactic breakdown. Stephen Greenblatt points out that when Othello wins Desdemona by becoming a tale of himself, he therefore ceases to be himself (Greenblatt, 238). (Sir Philip Sidney's lovesick persona in the sonnet sequence 'Astrophil and Stella' also turns himself into narrative when he asks his beloved to 'pity the tale of me'; sonnet 45). As we shall see in Chapter 3, Othello is not a person but a narrative, an epic hero, a fiction.

In Act Four, after Othello has struck Desdemona, the conversation between Desdemona and Montano is about who Othello 'is'. Lodovico asks, 'Is this the noble Moor?' (4.1.264); 'is it his use?' [i.e. is this violence his custom?] Montano has earlier posed a similar question about Cassio and alcohol, 'But is he often thus?' [i.e. is he regularly drunk?] (2.3.124). Whereas in Act Two Iago had answered Montano with an outright lie, saying Cassio gets drunk every night, in Act Four his response to Lodovico is riddling:

> He's that he is: I may not breathe my censure
> What he might be; if what he might, he is not,
> I would to heaven he were!

> (4.1.270–2)

He follows this with a more specific statement about identity. Lodovico shall watch Othello and thus see what he 'is': 'You shall observe him / And his own courses will denote him' (4.1.279–80). Both statements are effective: Lodovico is no longer able to think what he previously thought about who Othello 'is'. His exit line is, 'I am sorry that I am deceived in him' (4.1.282).

And so this brings us to Othello's request in Act Five. How do we tidy shifting, discontinuous identity into narrative? Is the analeptic story in Othello's speech to the Senate in Act

One, covering what happened and who he is up to this point, any more true a summary than that which he proposes at the moment of death? (*Analepsis* is the technical term for 'the narration of an event at a point later than its chronological place in a story; ... a flashback'; *OED* 4). How close is his Senate speech to this identity, given that we watch him telling a story about himself telling a story? How close is any of his rhetoric to his identity given that he begins and ends in story-telling? Is his Act Five summary an attempt not to formulate identity but to reassert control over narrative, a world that has, for five acts, been in Iago's control? Is it an optimism that, in death, words and subject ('me') can be united?

Postmortem meaning

We looked above at attempts to tidy the self posthumously in narrative at the end of other Shakespeare tragedies. But we looked only at plays, omitting to consider one of Shakespeare's earliest tragedies, the narrative poem *The Rape of Lucrece*. In this work, a decade before *Othello*, Shakespeare is alert to the difficulty of speaking of someone as they are.

Lucrece, the wife of Collatine, has been raped by the king's son, Sextus Tarquinius. (This event leads to revolt, the abolition of the monarchy, and the establishment of the Roman republic in 509 BCE.) When Shakespeare's Lucrece anticipates the public shame of her violation by Tarquin, she foresees it as a narrative infamy:

> The nurse to still her child will tell my story,
> And fright her crying babe with TARQUIN's name.
> The orator to deck his oratory
> Will couple my reproach to TARQUIN's shame.
> Feast-finding minstrels, tuning my defame,
>   Will tie the hearers to attend each line,
>   How TARQUIN wronged me, I COLLATINE.

(813–19)

Keen to take control of the narrative, Lucrece resists suicide until she has had the chance to speak of herself as she is to her husband (Collatine) and her father (Lucretius). Then, naming her violator, she sheathes the knife 'in her harmless breast' (1723).

What follows, however, is a competition between two males for sorrow – and for ownership of the meaning of Lucrece's body and narrative:

> The one doth call her his, the other his,
> Yet neither may possess the claim they lay.
> The father says, 'She's mine'. 'O, mine she is',
> Replies her husband: 'do not take away
> My sorrow's interest; let no mourner say
>   He weeps for her, for she was only mine,
>   And only must be wailed by COLLATINE'.

(1793–9)

Similar rivalry in grief occurs at the end of *Romeo and Juliet*, written the year after *The Rape of Lucrece*. The surviving Montague and Capulet families compete in providing the richest memorials to the dead teenagers. Capulet, Juliet's father, asks for a handshake of peace. Romeo's father offers 'more / For I will raise her statue in pure gold'; Capulet responds, 'As rich shall Romeo's by his lady's lie' (5.3.298–9, 303). Productions sometimes indicate the uselessness, or even the hollowness, of these gestures; Michael Bogdanov's production for the Royal Shakespeare Company in 1986 had the feuding families reconcile for the TV cameras, hurriedly dropping their handshakes the moment the cameras stopped rolling. This was a production that exposed the fiscal basis of Veronese society throughout and so obviously saw two gold statues at the end as evidence that nothing had changed. But one need not go this far to see the clear-eyed reality in these speeches: rather than showing further fiscal rivalry they may be simply an attempt to establish meaning in death – the predicament we see in *The Rape of Lucrece* and *Othello*.

Speaking of the deceased as they are is not about accurately representing their life but about trying to establish meaning in their death. In the cases of *Lucrece* and *Romeo and Juliet*, the concern is to provide a civic or political meaning that will lead to peace and stability. The narrative becomes a substitute with its own separate purpose: not commemoration but forward-planning, not how 'I am' (or they are) but the best that narrative can do at this moment. (I am grateful to the under-graduate students whose observations led to this paragraph.)

To 'speak of me as I am' is an invitation to summarize 'reputation'. This is the narrative problem Cassio wrestles with in Act Two: in losing his reputation he exchanges a good narrative about what he is for a bad. And that narrative of ontology ('ontology' is the nature of being) is not based on what he is but on what he has done (done only once – been drunk) translated into narrative: 'I will ask him for my place again, he shall tell me I am a drunkard' (2.3.298–9). 'I *am* a drunkard': what he has *done* has quickly become what he *is*. Reputation is not what you are, but what others say about you. The best Othello can hope for is not truth or transparency (what 'I am') but paradox – 'an honourable murderer', a combination of the ongoing self and the one-off criminal deed.

Othello ends, then, as it began, with a wedge, with meaning prised apart, with two meanings in one. This is the problem of language. And the play's problem is that Iago has not just recognized it as a problem but elevated it to a strategy. He decouples the self 'as I am' from outward signs. The gap he opens up, he fills with (false) interpretation, false meaning.

Language and comedy

This kind of linguistic separation is (like narrative above) never a problem in comedy. This is partly because comedy instantly identifies the problem. In *The Two Gentlemen of Verona* one of the comic servants, Speed, recognizes his companion servant's tactic: 'well, your old vice still: mistake the word' (3.1.278).

Twelfth Night, a comedy written a few years before *Othello* (or, in Honigmann's analysis, the same year; see Honigmann ed., 344–50) foregrounds the same themes and language as the tragedy. When Viola describes Feste as the fool, she commends his wit, his powers of observation, his opportunism, his timing. She could be describing Iago:

> This fellow is wise enough to play the fool,
> And to do that well craves a kind of wit.
> He must observe their mood on whom he jests,
> The quality of persons, and the time,
> And, like the haggard [hunting bird], check at every
>   feather
> That comes before his eye. This is a practice
> As full of labour as a wise man's art
> For folly that he wisely shows is fit.

(3.1.58–65)

Early in the play Viola is asked if she is a comedian [actor]. She answers, Iago-like, 'No, ... and yet ... I am not that that I play' (1.5.178–9). The collocation is similar to Iago's but the sentiments are reversed: Iago plays not that he is. Iago's riddling often involves the verb 'to be': in Act One he tells Roderigo 'Were I the Moor, I would not be Iago' (1.1.56). This kind of riddle about exchange of identity is typical of comedy and has a long history: in *The Lady of Andros*, a comedy by the ancient Roman playwright Terence (c. 185–159 BCE], one character says, 'if you were I, you'd think differently' [*'tu si hic sis, aliter sensias'*] (I.32–3).

The frequency with which this chapter invokes comedy indicates the difficulty of continuing our discussion without confronting an issue that is unavoidable in *Othello* criticism – the question of the play's mixed genre: *Othello* is a play that begins in comedy and ends in tragedy. In the next chapter we shall investigate this familiar and important topic and resituate it not just in structure and content but also in language.

Writing matters

- *Othello* is full of stories within stories. We have looked at some of them – Othello's wooing of Desdemona, for example, retold to the Senate; Iago's account of the brawl on guard duty in Cyprus. What is the *dramatic* effect of a play that contains so much *narrative*?

- We get glimpses of other stories. The untold narrative of Desdemona's mother with her divided duty is hinted at but dropped ('What's her history?' – 'A blank'; *Twelfth Night* 2.4.110). (Those interested in creative writing might like to write a first-person history of Othello's mother.) We know a lot about Othello's background; we know very little indeed about Iago's background (beyond one startlingly specific detail, his age: see Introduction). Make a list of all the things the play tells us about Othello's life experience (e.g. his royal ancestry, his captivity, his life spent in military camps until nine months previously, etc.) and the facts you can infer from these details. Make a list of everything that the play tells us about Iago's background (this will be a much shorter list). Now extend your lists to include each character's wife – what do we know about Desdemona and what do we know about Emilia? – and about each pair of characters as a couple. (For an example of how an actress approached the relative dearth of information about Emilia see Amanda Harris' excellent essay in *Performing Shakespeare's Tragedies Today* in which she describes how she and her Iago (Antony Sher) tried to fill in the couple's back story. Carol Rutter's chapter in *Enter the Body* offers an analysis of female bonding in an RSC production directed by Trevor Nunn and available on DVD). Why do you think Shakespeare gives us so much information about Othello (and his wife) and so little about Iago (and his wife)? What is the effect on us as readers/audience members of knowing so much about one pair of characters and so little about the other? Finally – read Shakespeare's source for the play, Cinthio's short novella, and make a list of all the details about Iago that Shakespeare omits and all the details about Othello that Shakespeare adds. Why do you think he altered the source in this way?

● Read Iago's description of Cassio at 2.1. 239–2. Using this as a departure point, note who controls naming in the play, who defines or inscribes other theatrical bodies. (You might also like to read Emma Smith's *TLS* review of Nicholas Hytner's production of *Othello* at London's National Theatre in 2013. Smith complained that Iago's 'world-view shapes much of what we see' and so the characters performed the roles 'prescribed for them by their ensign director'.)

● Look at embedded or implicit stage directions (from 'thus' to Iago's misleading descriptions of other characters). What is the relation between the verbal and visual means of telling a story in this play (and is it an interrelation or a conflict?) It looks like it is always Iago who is presenting the story – how does this affect our awareness of right and wrong interpretations?

● Think about the ways that selfhood and autobiography are presented in narrative:

a) If you are interested in classical rhetoric read Peter Dixon's excellent (short) book on *Rhetoric* (1971) and identify the technical stages of Othello's self-presentation to the Senate at

1.3.129–71, noting what effect they have or are designed to have. (Dixon's book is out of print but is available in most libraries. You might also like to consult Chapter 1 of Richard Toye's *Rhetoric: A Very Short Introduction* (2013); and see also *Classical Rhetoric for the Modern Student* by Edward P. J. Corbett and P. J. Connors (1998))

b) Compare Othello's presentation to the Senate in Act One with other narratives of self-presentation in Shakespeare: Egeon's autobiography to the Duke in Act One of *Comedy of Errors* and Prospero's autobiography to Miranda in Act One of *The Tempest*. What do these two narratives have in common? Is it significant that these accounts are presented at the *beginning* of the plays? That they occur in comedies? What is the difference between these and Othello's brief autobiographical account at the end of *Othello*? What is the difference between Othello's long account to the Senate at the start of the play and his brief account at the end?

CHAPTER TWO

Language and genre

Genre is usually thought about in relation to plot rather than language. Lines by the Romantic poet, Lord Byron, are the most invoked (because so neatly aphoristic):

All tragedies are finished by a death
All comedies are ended by a marriage.

(*Don Juan* III.9.1–2)

This is the premise that motivates Marc Foster's Hollywood film *Stranger than Fiction* (2006) in which a tax inspector, Harold Crick (Will Ferrell) hears a voice narrating his story, a story that ends in death. Refusing to believe his therapist's diagnosis of schizophrenia, he consults a university professor of English, Jules Hilbert (Dustin Hoffman). Hilbert suspects that Crick is a character in a novel, not a schizophrenic; and a linguistic clue – the dramatic irony inherent in the omniscient voice's phrase, 'little did he know ...' – helps him identify the tragic genre in which the story of Harold's life is taking place. Quoting Italo Calvino rather than Byron on the distinction between comedy's 'continuity' and tragedy's 'inevitability of death', Hilbert explains: 'in tragedy you die, in comedy you get hitched'. In order to prevent the omniscient narrator killing Harold off, he urges Harold to 'develop' the potential for comedy in his life. (Enter Maggie Gylenhaal as a free-thinking, tax-withholding baker whose tax returns Harold has to investigate. Hilbert finds her initial antagonism promising generically as a convention of romantic comedy.)

Taking control of your life's genre is also the premise behind Tim Minchin's lyrics for *Matilda the Musical* (2010). Analysing tragic endings from Jack and Jill to *Romeo and Juliet*, Matilda sings:

> The endings are often a little bit gory.
> I wonder why they didn't just change their story.

She realizes that 'nobody else is gonna put it right for me. / Nobody but me is gonna change my story'. By manipulating the plot, tragic endings can be averted.

This is what Susan Snyder has called the 'evitability principle'. You will not find 'evitability' in the *OED*; this is Snyder's coinage, from analogy with the word 'inevitability'. (Or perhaps 'inevitability' is a fossil word, like 'feckless', 'unkempt', 'disgruntled', where English retains the negative form when the positive term becomes obsolete.) 'Inevitability' comes from Latin; the negating prefix *in* is simply attached to *evitabilis*, avoidable. In English if we want to say that something is avoidable, we have to use the word I have just used (a Middle English word from Anglo-Norman, *avoider*) rather than the Latinate *evitable*. But Snyder's neologism (coinage; literally, new word) is helpful in talking about drama because it foregrounds a structural difference between the genres of comedy and tragedy: in comedy catastrophe can be averted – is 'evitable' – and the forward momentum of negative, potentially tragic, forces can be redirected. A bad brother and a usurping duke can be converted in *As You Like It*. The machinations of the disaffected Don John can be foiled in *Much Ado*. A lost family can be found, a thousand ducats obtained and a death sentence reversed in *Comedy of Errors*. A dead brother can be found alive in *Twelfth Night*. A blocking figure, Duke Theseus, can sanction Hermia's choice of husband in *Midsummer Night's Dream* and although her father does not give his blessing in Act Five, he is not given lines in which to register any continued objection. (In fact, he may not even be present at all since his lines appear only in the 1623 Folio; they are given to Philostrate in the 1600 Quarto.) In comedy, tragic threat is always 'evitable' whereas in tragedy the threat moves towards an unavoidable conclusion. As the chorus observes in Jean Anouilh's tragedy, *Antigone* (1942):

> So. Now the spring is wound. The tale will unfold all of itself. That's the convenient thing about tragedy – you can start it off with the flick of a finger. … That's all it takes. And afterwards, no need to do anything. It does itself. Like clockwork set going since the beginning of time. Death, treachery, despair – all there ready and waiting.
>
> (Anouilh, 101)

Generic fluidity

Byron's couplet is prescriptive. In fact, genre was more fluid in earlier periods than it is for us. The ancient Greeks had only three dramatic categories into which to slot plays – comedy, tragedy and satyr-play. Consequently the categories were capacious: Euripides' tragedies encompass what we would now call tragicomedy. (This is worth remembering as Shakespeare is, in many ways, a very Euripidean writer – in his treatment of women, his plots, and his mixing of genres). Stephen Orgel writes that 'Genres for us are exclusive and definitive, whereas for the Renaissance they tended to be inclusive and relational' (Orgel ed. *Winter's Tale*, 3). Alastair Fowler uses an analogy from the paint chart: genres, like colours, operate on a spectrum, overlapping and blending into each other: 'in their strong tints they are easily distinguished; but are susceptible of so much variety, and take on so many different forms, that we can never say where one species ends and another begins' (Fowler, 37). Elsewhere Fowler uses an image from the photo album, talking of genres as family members 'related in various ways, without necessarily having any single feature shared by all' (Fowler, 41). Genres are thus not fixed entities. Genre is the pigeon not the pigeonhole (Fowler, 37). It is something that moves, not something that has come home to roost.

Jonathan Hope and Michael Witmore say something similar. Genre is dynamic:

> a transaction between a spectator and a company ... Perhaps rather than a recipe or essence, theatrical genre is really an oscillation between certain generic possibilities at a given moment in time.
>
> (Hope and Witmore, 375)

As we shall see later in this chapter, language is one way of signalling 'generic possibilities'.

Juxtaposing genres

Shakespeare juxtaposed genres within plays from the start of his career. A death threat hangs over Egeon for five acts in *Comedy of Errors*; marriages are postponed at the end of *Love's Labour's Lost*; *Romeo and Juliet* begins with brawling servants and bawdy males, and has an urban mercantile setting throughout – these are very much the domains of comedy. Even a so-called 'happy' comedy like the mature *Twelfth Night* is full of references to and reminders of death (Elam, ed. *Twelfth Night*, 56–7). Shakespeare rarely keeps the comic and tragic worlds apart.

This generic mixing is not confined to a comic/tragic binary. *Troilus and Cressida* takes heroic Greek material – the Trojan war – and submits it to a Roman treatment: satire. *Coriolanus*, writes Lois Potter, 'is tragicomedy in the fullest sense of the word: the desire for tragic grandeur is constantly undercut by an apparent inability to believe in it' (Potter 2012, 349).

When Shakespeare's colleagues in the King's Men theatre company, John Heminge and Henry Condell, edited his complete plays for posthumous publication (the volume was published in 1623, seven years after Shakespeare's death), the title page advertises the book not as *Shakespeare's Plays* nor as *Shakespeare's Works* but as *Mr William Shakespeare's Comedies, Histories & Tragedies*. Similarly, the book's contents page gives 'a catalogue of the severall Comedies, Histories, and Tragedies contained in this Volume'. If you look at the contents, you will see that Shakespeare's canon is evenly divided across these three genres. This is unusual and I think Heminge and Condell wanted to draw attention to this fact. Ben Jonson wrote two (extant) tragedies but neither was a success in his own day nor are they regularly revived in ours. For Jonson, tragedy was not 'a genuine artistic alternative' to comedy (Barton, 156); his talent (and fame) lay in satirical city comedy. Although Thomas Middleton wrote in several genres, his canon contains only three great tragedies and again, like Jonson, his contemporary success lay in city comedy. Shakespeare was generically trilingual. It should therefore come as no surprise to find a writer fluid in three genres mixing genres within a single play.

Comedy is generally a world without pain – or a world in which pain has no long-term effects or consequences. As Shakespeare develops in comedic technique, he becomes more interested in pushing the boundary between comedy and tragedy. Characters are excluded from the harmonious conclusions of *Merchant of Venice* (Shylock), *Twelfth Night* (Malvolio), *Much Ado about Nothing* (Don John); in the tragicomic *Winter's Tale*, Mamillius dies and nothing can restore him (or the lost 16 years of marriage and parenthood). Othello contributes to this on-going experiment in comedy. It is an essay in Beyond Comedy, an exploration of what happens to the world of comedy (with which *Othello* opens) if its pledge of psychic immunity is betrayed. In the last scene of the 2013 National Theatre production, Rory Kinnear's Iago stared incredulously open-mouthed at the 'tragic loading of this bed' (5.2.361); he had never envisaged his trickery going this far and having such consequences.

Generic mixing is obvious from the beginning of *Othello*. The play begins with an elopement, the standard material of comedy: think of the lovers Hermia and Lysander in *Midsummer Night's Dream*, Silvia and Valentine in *Two Gentlemen of Verona*, Jessica and Lorenzo in *Merchant of Venice*. (Oliver Parker's film of *Othello* actually shows the elopement and marriage: it begins with a late night gondola escape and hurried journeying towards a secret wedding ceremony.) The marriage couples an older man with a younger woman – again, traditional comic fare. Iago convinces Othello that he is a cuckold (the cuckold plot is one of the oldest comic structures). The husband is generally a comic, not a tragic, identity. Comedy is often put under pressure when a man marries. When David Suchet observes that 'Iago is a man whose life has changed through his general's marriage' (Suchet, 187) it is hard not to think of *Merchant of Venice* or *Much Ado About Nothing*, comedies in which male friendship is affected when one man changes status from bachelor to husband. Antonio tries to articulate his sadness in the first scene of *Merchant of Venice* as his friend Bassanio embarks on a wooing quest; the males in *Much Ado* tease Benedick when he detaches himself from the group of bachelor males to form a new alliance with Beatrice. One of the first things that Iago tells us is that he has served in battle with Othello 'at Rhodes, at Cyprus and on other grounds / Christian and heathen' (1.1.29–30). The military advisor who worked with the cast on the 2013 National Theatre production in London cautions us not to underestimate the implications of these lines: it is likely that Iago has saved Othello's life and vice versa; they have been allies in conditions of extreme crisis and threat. Such shared experience creates very deep links – a link that is now broken by Othello's marriage (Shaw, programme article).

Critics and actors have identified Iago as a puppet-master or a trickster or a commedia dell'arte improvisor or a character who proceeds by low cunning rather than intelligence – all comic traditions. But as Douglas Bruster observes, Iago does not know the rules of the comic plot he is creating: that comedy does not do death (Bruster, 106).

The generic juxtapositions continue. The scene in which Othello treats Emilia as a brothel-keeper (4.2) is a twisted import from city comedy (that satiric Jacobean form that staged sexual intrigues and mercantile appetites). The conversation in which Emilia and Desdemona ponder Othello's anger results in Emilia trying to fit Othello's behaviour within a genre: the genre of domestic comedy in which household tensions erupt in violence (4.3.85–102). When Iago reassures Roderigo that things will work out to Roderigo's benefit, he says 'Wit depends on dilatory time' (i.e. cleverness needs time; 2.3.368). Dilatory time is the property of comedy, not tragedy. Desdemona is given two sequential death scenes, one in which she resists and vociferously plea-bargains for an extension of her life (5.1.77–83) and one in which she acquiesces, accepting responsibility for her death (5.1.122–3); the former belongs to comedy, the latter to tragedy.

Desdemona belongs linguistically to comedy in the way she insistently pleads to her husband for Cassio. In this she flouts all the contemporary conduct-book rules for the dutiful wife (who should not interfere in her husband's business affairs and who should take her cue for conversation and mood from his desires and demeanour). But Desdemona's insistence takes her yet further – into the comic territory of the shrew:

> My lord shall never rest,
> I'll watch him tame, and talk him out of patience;
> His bed shall seem a school, his board a shrift.

> (3.3.22–4)

Keeping one's husband awake with nagging ('I'll watch him tame'), disrupting his rest ('bed') and his meals ('board') are stereotypical shrew actions. So too is not letting a subject drop. Othello wants to speak 'some other time' (3.355); Desdemona does not accept this vague promise and presses for

specificity ('But shall't be shortly? ... tonight? ... tomorrow?';
56–8). Even when she has got her own way, with Othello
promising to talk to Cassio, Desdemona persists, justifying her
behaviour as being for Othello's benefit (3.376–83). These are
artless and loving repetitions; but a contemporary audience
would recognize their generic origins in comedy.

One of the striking features of *Othello* is the way that the
plot could conceivably be comedy (and has the potential to
move to a comedic resolution) until very late in the action.
When Iago says 'But let her live' (3.3.477), this is the moment
at which we first glimpse the alternative possibility – that
Desdemona might not live (Leggatt, 123).

Props

From plot to props. *Othello* is unusual among Shakespeare
tragedies in its focus on a prop: the handkerchief. This
distressed the seventeenth-century writer, Thomas Rymer,
who, in *A Short View of Tragedy* (1693) complained that
the prop was a 'trifle' which could not support the tragic
weight given it. He offered what he saw as a more logical
textile alternative: 'had it been Desdemona's Garter, the
Sagacious Moor might have smelt a Rat' (Rymer, 159). No
other Shakespeare tragedy is dependent on a material prop.
(In fact, actors regularly note, when assembling the props for
performances of *Othello*, that if they forget the handkerchief,
there would be no tragedy.) Trevor Nunn's Royal Shakespeare
Company production of 1989 exploited this in his staging of
3.3, the scene in which Desdemona drops her handkerchief
after having tried to use it to bind Othello's head. Imogen
Stubbs' Desdemona exited with Othello, solicitously attending
to her husband ('I am very sorry that you are not well';
3.3.293), only to return immediately to retrieve a forgotten
item – Othello's pocket watch which he had left on the desk.
Audience members familiar with the play gasped as they

looked at the forgotten handkerchief, now twice neglected, on the floor beneath and registered the closeness with which the tragedy had come to being averted.

Props are the property of comedy. *Comedy of Errors* has a bag of ducats, a necklace, a rope. Romances are dependent on a token to identify the noble origins of a foundling. In *The Winter's Tale* the baby Perdita is abandoned with 'gold' and 'a bearing cloth [christening robe] for a squire's child' (3.3.120, 114) that the Shepherd who finds her keeps in a 'fardel and box' (4.4.757); the items are produced in the reunion scene, although Shakespeare narrates their production rather than staging it. Although props in comedy get transferred or are lost or fall into the wrong hands, in all cases they end up in the right place. This does not happen to the handkerchief in *Othello*.

Othello and Ben Jonson

Although the original audience would have expected *Othello* to be a tragedy (both from its being advertised as such and from the black hangings with which the stage was decorated for tragedies), they may well have associated the play with comedy for reasons outside the play. Ben Jonson had named a character Thorello in his recent play for Shakespeare's company, *Every Man In his Humour* (1598). This jealous husband was a character in a comedy; the audience could not have missed the striking resemblance with the similarly named Othello (played by the same actor, Richard Burbage, who had played Thorello). Jealous husbands are comic figures: Shakespeare had dramatized one only a few years previously, Master Ford in *Merry Wives of Windsor*. In the character of Ford, Shakespeare does what he will do again with the character of Leontes in *The Winter's Tale*: he collapses the Iago and the Othello figures into one. Both Ford and Leontes goad themselves into jealousy. In *Othello* Shakespeare separates the two personalities, the tormentor and the tormented, into two – Iago provokes, Othello is provoked – and (consequently?) changes the genre into tragedy.

The relation between Jonson's *Every Man In* and *Othello* is seen in more than just plot and similarity of character name. *Othello* repeatedly references the earlier Jonson play. Contemplating his wife's possible infidelity, Thorello reasons:

> if I but thought the time
> Had answered their affections, all the world
> Should not persuade me but I were a cuckold.

> (1.4.174–6)

Shakespeare takes this comment on time scheme and probability and places it at the heart of his tragedy where Othello never questions the time or the circumstance.

In *Every Man In*, Thorello agonizes, 'What meant I to marry?' (3.3.15–19). At a similar juncture, Othello asks 'Why did I marry?' (3.3.245). In *Every Man In*, Thorello calms a quarrel with 'Put up your weapons and put off this rage' (3.4.163), lines that *Othello* recycles in Act One: 'Keep up your bright swords' (1.2.59). In *Every Man In*, Oliver Cob boasts 'I do fetch my pedigree and name from the first red herring' (1.3.13–14); Shakespeare's Othello has a similar speech with a grander pedigree (1.2.21–2).

Shakespeare was later to see the tragic potential in a comic plot when the profligate hero of Thomas Middleton's comedy *A Mad World, My Masters* (1606), Sir Bounteous Prodigal, was transformed into a tragic protagonist, the bounteous prodigal of the collaborative tragedy *Timon of Athens* (1607) by Shakespeare and Middleton. (The generic initiative in this collaborative work may have been Middleton's as much as Shakespeare's; see Maguire and Smith 2012.)

But the dialogue between *Every Man In* and *Othello* does not stop with the writing of *Othello*. Immediately after *Othello* was written and performed, Jonson put a jealous husband, Corvino, into his comedy, *Volpone* (1605). As my colleague Margaret Tudeau-Clayton points out, it is as if Jonson is pointedly saying to Shakespeare: '*this* is the genre in which jealous husbands belong'. Jonson's view is also behind Rymer's unease with the materials of this play: Othello's 'Love and his Jealousie are no part of a Souldier's Character, unless for Comedy' (Rymer, 134).

Othello and Christopher Marlowe

Othello's generic experimentation is not linked to a simple opposition (structural or linguistic) between comedy and tragedy. Philip Brockbank finds in *Othello* a play that speaks two languages: Othello's 'heroic and magnanimous view of life' versus Iago's 'harsh and colloquial' view in which Iago performs 'front-stage, holding the audience in a cynical acceptance of what human nature boils down to' (Brockbank, 205). Here, then, we have two registers and two stage techniques. But Brockbank complicates simple attempts at contrastive pairing by showing the diverse generic traditions that come together in *Othello*: pageant, miracle play (drama about a saint's life), morality play, history, heroic tragedy. Many of these genres (the first three in this list, for instance) are medieval in origin, although they had a stage life in the English provinces until the late sixteenth century.

Morality drama is moral and spiritual in its aims and its main characters are allegorical figures. The Vice figure is morality drama's chief comic character; his role is to lead the hero astray. Many critics have noted Iago's derivation from the morality tradition: a Vice figure whose relationship with the audience is developed in confidential and confessional dialogue with us. This is the allegorical tradition that Othello has in mind when at the end he seeks Iago's cloven feet (5.2.283), assuming that only a devil could have behaved as Iago did: 'demand that demi-devil / Why he hath thus ensnared my soul and body' (5.2.298–9). In considering Othello as a heroic character and Iago as a Vice figure, Brockbank identifies both a generic common denominator and a clash between the two traditions: both Othello and Iago are ambitious but ambition is a virtue in the heroic tradition and a vice (indeed, as Brockbank punningly points out, a Vice) in the morality tradition (Brockbank, 204).

If *Othello* is indebted to medieval generic tradition, it also has a more immediate linguistic source in the plays of Shakespeare's contemporary, Christopher Marlowe (1564–93). Marlowe burst onto the English dramatic scene in the late 1580s with a new kind of drama. His heroes *sounded* different: they speak in iambic pentameter. Blank [unrhymed] verse on stage, which we recognize as the staple of Elizabethan drama, is actually Marlowe's innovation. His characters are also rhetorically hypnotic. Marlowe's first hero, Tamburlaine, astounds us with his hyperbolic images and mythological allusions, his incantatory repetitions, and his extravagant geographical references. His speech affects not just those on stage who listen to him (he conquers in part just by opening his mouth whereupon people switch to his side) but those in the London theatre world: most dramatists of the 1590s set about trying to copy the Tamburlaine style.

We can see Marlowe's influence on Othello's rhetoric. The mouth-filling rhodomontade of Tamburlaine becomes the exotic marine imagery or cosmic imagination of Othello:

> Like to the Pontic Sea
> Whose icy current and compulsive course
> Ne'er keeps retiring ebb but keeps due on
> To the Propontic and the Hellespont:
> Even so my bloody thoughts with violent pace
> Shall ne'er look back, ne'er ebb to humble love,
> Till that a capable and wide revenge
> Swallow them up.

> (3.3.456–63)

O insupportable, O heavy hour!
Methinks it should be now a huge eclipse
Of sun and moon, and that th' affrighted globe
Should yawn at alteration.

(5.2.99–110)

Brockbank links the medieval and the Marlovian in an argument that extends our generic inquiry. He suggests that the play poses the question: what happens to Tamburlaine and Zenocrate when Ambidexter gets to work on them? (Zenocrate is the wife of Marlowe's warrior-hero Tamburlaine; Ambidexter is the Vice-figure in Thomas Preston's late morality play, *Cambyses* (published 1569, written c. 1564), a play Shakespeare knew: he refers to it in *1 Henry IV*, 2.4.377; Brockbank, 203). In a parenthesis, Brockbank later offers an exclusively Marlovian parallel, invoking the tricksters of Marlowe's tragicomic *Jew of Malta*: 'Othello has arrived in the theatre of the devil and the double-dealer (it is as if Tamburlaine comes to the Malta of Marlowe's Barabas and Ithamore)' (Brockbank, 209). There is a complex interconnectedness in all Brockbank's allusions but they are simply variant attempts to articulate a generic contrast, whether between periods of drama, types of drama, types of language or types of character, all of which come together in *Othello*.

Another critic contrasts Othello's heroic way of thinking with the world in which he finds himself. In Act Three Othello says:

                    I had rather be a toad
And live upon the vapour of a dungeon
Than keep a corner in a thing I love
For others' uses.

(3.3.274–7)

John Turner comments, 'This dream of sterile perfection is a dream of art, more specifically of Romance. It is the imposition on the world of a particular kind of story and an attempt to live it, an attempt which proves fatal' (Holderness, Potter and Turner, 188). The absolute Romance visions of Othello and Desdemona conflict with the expediency of the early modern Venetian city. Here Turner offers a different kind of generic contrast, one which also has two different languages: the fictional world of romance values and the fiscal world of city values.

The collision of traditions and world views is perhaps most obvious in the linguistic clash of Act 5, scene 2. Othello's heroic imagination sees the sacrifice/murder in cosmic terms (quoted above). This is a continuation of Othello's tendency to use images of the moon: 'as fresh as Dian's visage' (3.1.389–90); 'It is the very error of the moon, / She comes nearer earth than she was wont' (5.2.108–9). We are in the heroic vein still, the world of tragedy. But Emilia will not acknowledge this genre and will only allow Othello 'a domestic disaster' (Brockbank, 216): 'O gull, O dolt, / As ignorant as dirt' (5.2.159).

It is worth pursuing Emilia's vocabulary here. Although our discussion above indicates that genre is more typically associated with plot than with language, Brockbank has introduced us to the concept of genre as linguistic through general association with Marlovian rhetoric. As we shall now see, *Othello* foregrounds the relationship between genre and language in three very specific lexical ways.

'Gull'

The first is through a single word, 'gull'. In Act Five, Emilia rounds on Othello: he is a dupe ('gull'), an idiot ('dolt'); later in this scene Emilia calls him a 'coxcomb' (fool) and a 'fool' (5.2.231). These are hardly nouns associated with a tragic hero.

Four other Shakespeare characters are called gulls. In *Henry V*, Gower describes Pistol as 'a gull, a fool, a rogue'

(3.6.66). In *Twelfth Night*, Malvolio is twice designated a gull: 'yond gull Malvolio' (3.2.66) and 'the most notorious geck [fool] and gull' (5.1.342); the similarly duped Sir Andrew Aguecheek is accused of being 'an ass-head, and a coxcomb, and a knave, a thin-fac'd knave, a gull!' (5.1.204–5). The Senator in *Timon of Athens* anticipates that 'Lord Timon will be left a naked gull / Which flashes now a phoenix' (2.1.31–2). In all these examples the noun is coded as Comedy. Pistol is a comic character, as are Malvolio and Sir Andrew; Timon may be a tragic hero but, as several critics have observed, he exists in a structure borrowed from city comedy (Maguire and Smith, 189–93).

Outside Shakespearean drama, the noun 'gull' appears almost exclusively in comedies. The list is long; a selective list (bracketed dates are those of first publication) includes Anon, *Wily Beguiled* (1606), Lording Barry's *Ram Alley* (1611), George Chapman's *All Fools* (1605), Chapman, Jonson and John Marston's *Eastward Ho!* (1605), several comedies by Chapman: *May Day* (1611), *Monsieur D'Olive* (1606), *A Humorous Day's Mirth* (1599), John Day's *Isle of Gulls* (1606) and *Law Tricks* (1608), Thomas Dekker and Thomas Middleton's *The Honest Whore* (1604), several comedies by Dekker: *Old Fortunatus* (1600), *Patient Grissill* (1603), *Satiromastix* (1602), *The Shoemaker's Holiday* (1600), Thomas Heywood's *Fair Maid of the Exchange* (1641), several comedies by Jonson: *The Case is Altered* (1609), *Every Man Out of his Humour* (1600), *Every Man In his Humour* (1601), *Cynthia's Revels* (1601), Marston's *Jack Drum's Entertainment* (1611) and *What You Will* (1607), Middleton's *Michaelmas Term* (1607). (Don't be misled by databases that bring up *King Lear*; Lear's complaint that his Fool is 'a pestilent gull to me' is the Quarto compositor's misprint for 'gall'; Q 1608, sig. C4v.) In the list above, note not only the consistency of comic genre but the cluster of dates in the first decade of the seventeenth century: 'gull' is a noun associated with comedies at the time Shakespeare was writing *Othello*.

'Gull' is also a concept associated with the popular coney-catching pamphlets of the period. Coney-catching (literally: rabbit-catching, hence the catching of an innocent) pamphlets are tales of thieving through trickery. An amoral rogue-hero uses his local knowledge to dupe a visitor who is unfamiliar in the ways and the words of a place.

Here genre interfaces with the topic of story-telling we explored in Chapter 1. Othello invests his selfhood in oratory and the equation between speech and behaviour. (We recall the view, expressed by numerous Roman rhetoricians who were studied in the early modern schoolroom, that oratory and morals are linked: an orator is 'a good man who speaks well' ['vir bonum, dicendi peritus'].) Consequently, Othello is out of his depth when he deals with Iago to whom behaviour and words are 'but sign' (1.1.155). Othello the orator is reduced to a gull as the world of classical rhetoric collides with the amorality of coney-catching where verbal skill is devoid of ethical import.

'Is't possible'?

A second lexical tic is the repeated question, 'Is't possible?' This question occurs no fewer than five times in *Othello*. When the sobered-up Cassio cannot remember why he quarrelled with Roderigo, Iago asks 'Is't possible?' (2.3.283). He asks the same of Othello when Othello gives his 'Farewell the tranquil mind' speech at 3.3.350ff. Desdemona later asks the question of Othello when he narrates the magical origin of the handkerchief at 3.4.70. When Iago goads Othello into a fit in Act Four with choice prepositional allusions to Cassio's sexual activity ('with her, on her'), Othello imagines the couple's closeness ('noses, ears and lips'), then asks 'Is't possible?' (4.1.42). Its final occurrence comes in 4.2 when Desdemona denies that she is a whore. 'What, not a whore?' asks Othello. 'Is't possible?' (4.2.88–9).

Sometimes the question is a logical response to a statement (as in Cassio's oblivion or Desdemona's denial). But at other times, such as Iago's response to Othello's speech or in Othello's own disintegrated syntax, the interrogative seems more a generic marker to us, the audience, perhaps even a surrogate for what we are cued to ask repeatedly in generic disbelief: how has this situation become possible? It is an interrogative formulation of Susan Snyder's evitability principle. It seems an innocuous phrase but its five occurrences in *Othello* contrast with its paucity of use elsewhere in the Shakespeare canon. Other plays usually extend the phrase and give it a specific application: 'Is it possible that love should of a sudden take such hold?' asks Tranio in *Taming of the Shrew* (1.1.146–7); 'Is it possible / A cur can lend three thousand ducats?' queries Shylock in *Merchant of Venice* (1.3.116–17). Where plays do give it a line to itself, as in *Twelfth Night* (3.4.127), *Troilus and Cressida* (4.2.76), *Much Ado about Nothing* (1.1.69) and *Julius Caesar* (4.3.38), the question has only a single occurrence in the play.

'No remedy'

Another linguistic generic marker relates to an even more inconspicuous phrase, 'no remedy'. In an as yet unpublished work, James Toole analyses the use of this phrase in texts from the late Middle Ages to the 1640s. Etymologically, 'remedy' means redress, a cure (from Latin *mederi* to heal); its meaning in English was initially medical. Extended to mean cures for problems generally, it acquired a theological meaning (a remedy for sin) and then a legal meaning (reparation for a wrong incurred).

Toole noticed a peak of uses in the period 1530–1630 and he further noticed that, whereas before this period the three meanings were kept apart, Renaissance dramatists exploited the word's multiplicity. (For instance, theological remedy can

be superimposed on, or conflict with, legal remedy, negoti-
ating problems of justice or revenge or authority.) Toole's
brilliance was not just in chronicling the epithet's history but
in seeing how dramatists introduced a new usage in which
they cued audiences to recognize *remedy* and *no remedy*
as related to genre. In short, comedy provides remedies –
situations are redressed, cured; they are 'evitable' – whereas
tragedy has no remedy. As Toole explains it, 'The presence or
absence of remedy constitutes a dramatics of expectation – we
are metatheatrically aware that what we expect is contingent
upon what the generic structure of the work allows us to
expect.'

It is notable how often the phrase 'remedy' or 'no remedy'
appears in the first half of plays, cueing audiences generically. Toole draws our attention to Shakespeare's *Measure
for Measure* (another mixed-genre play, written at the same
time as *Othello*). A wise old lord accept the death sentence
given to the young Claudio: 'It grieves me for the death of
Claudio, / But there's no remedy' (2.1.267–8). Just a few lines
later, he repeats the sentiment: 'But yet, poor Claudio! There
is no remedy' (282). (This exchange is Thomas Middleton's
1621 revision to Shakespeare's text.) In the next scene, in
Shakespeare's writing, the heroine Isabella pleads with the
man who sentenced Claudio:

> *Isabella.*   Must he [Claudio] needs die?
> *Angelo.*   Maiden, no remedy.

(2.2.48)

Isabella fights back both theologically and generically: 'Yes: I
do think that you might pardon him, / And neither heaven nor
man grieve at the mercy' (2.2.49–50). If you provide a remedy,
she says, this will become a comedy.

Toole's argument is detailed and complex and it deserves
more space than I can give it here. But I cite it as an example
(one more example) of the subtle ways in which early modern
dramatists transacted linguistically with genre. We should

bear this in mind when *Othello* opens with Iago apparently accepting the tragic inevitability of his situation as Cassio's subordinate: 'Why, there's no remedy, 'tis the curse of service: / Preferment goes by letter and affection' (1.1.34–5). Here, for an audience, is the acoustic marker of genre: we are in a tragedy. (Or Iago is.) But Iago quickly decides to fight against his remediless situation, redirecting the play's genre to comedy. It is late in the play before it turns back to tragedy.

DocuScope

Another complex account of the relation between language and genre has recently been given by Jonathan Hope and Michael Witmore. Working with a computer analysis they propose that genre is visible lexically – at the level of the sentence (Hope and Witmore, 361).

The computer programme they use, DocuScope, is essentially a smart dictionary; it 'reads' strings of characters, looking for words, and collects any words that it recognizes (where 'recognize' means 'match'). The words and phrases (strings) that DocuScope has been programmed to identify have shorthand summary tags: Direct Address ('ye', 'thou'); Self Disclosure (when a noun or line from a character offers a personal revelation – 'my passion' – or a verb indicates a personal point of view – 'I think'); Refute That (a direct refutation: 'I deny that'); Deny Disclaim (a similar concept using a negative: 'There is no conspiracy'); Uncertainty (verbs like 'seems' and adverbs like 'perhaps' which indicate the subjective nature of the speaker's statement); First Person ('I', 'we'). (These examples come from Hope and Witmore, 360 and from Hope, 188–90.)

The above tags cluster in Comedies and are conspicuously absent from Histories, which have a different set of identifying markers: for instance, their DocuScope tags include: Inclusive ('our', invoking a sense of community or commonwealth);

Common Authority ('God', 'Lord'); Sense Objects (concrete nouns); Sense Property (adjectives). There is no reason why Comedy or History should not contain the linguistic markers of the other genre. The fact is, they don't. Linguistically, one genre not only avoids the markers of the other but is tantamount to being in opposition to it. Genres, in other words, have an 'empirical linguistic existence' (Hope, 191). DocuScope's generic division of the canon is easily visible on a graph, where, for example, Tragedy clusters in one quadrant and Comedy in another.

What is fascinating, graphically and linguistically, is that *Othello* appears on the graph as an outlier in the tragic quadrant, having more in common with the comedies. This is, of course, what literary critics have long recognized. Hope and Witmore do not claim that DocuScope offers critical objectivity so much as a quantified subjectivity. But they also suggest that literary critics who see *Othello* as comedic are responding at some level to the play's language as well as its structure.

As an example, they map a dialogue from *Othello* on to *Twelfth Night*. Act 3, scene 3 of *Othello* is the scene in which Iago draws Othello in and hooks him with indirections, allusions, cryptic comments, silence. Act 1, scene 5 of *Twelfth Night* is the scene in which the countess Olivia is drawn to an interest in the messenger Cesario (really Viola in disguise) by Cesario's evasive answers and indirections. Othello and Olivia are both trying 'to delve into the thoughts of [their] interlocutor'. Iago and Cesario are both 'refusing to give the speaker something he wants, and in doing so, goading the speaker on'. The Comic structure is 'the continued stance that allows a "withholding speaker" (Iago) and an eager listener (Othello) to push back and forth on one another ... The parallel is perverse, but it shows that a very different emotional trajectory can take shape on a similar linguistic footing' (Hope and Witmore, 377).

Later they argue that, in linguistic terms, Othello's confrontation of Desdemona – 'What art thou?' in 4.2 – has all the lexical hallmarks of a recognition scene. 'Like Viola declaring who she is to [her brother] Sebastian in *Twelfth Night*, Desdemona asserts who – not what – she is in the face of something like a disguise, forced upon her by Iago's accusations' (Hope and Witmore, 378). Recognition scenes conclude comedies. This one is not comic and it resolves things in the wrong direction.

Hope and Witmore's explanation leads to a number of interesting questions. 'How much "Comic" language can a Tragedy like *Othello* tolerate? … [W]hat does this type of linguistic borrowing say about the ways in which genre is staged, cued, and self-consciously manipulated by authors?' (382). This second question gets to the heart of Renaissance drama, which seems to be acutely self-conscious about genre.

Early modern plays regularly call attention to aspects of their structure or their audience's expectations. In *Richard II* Bolingbroke responds to frantic knocking at the door and a request for pardon with a recognition of the scene's sharp change in genre: 'Our scene is alter'd from a serious thing, / And now changed to 'The Beggar and the King' (the reference is to a ballad, and probably a Tudor interlude, of the name). *Richard III* is full of stagey, hammy references: 'And in good time, here comes the sweating lord' (3.1.24). In *King Lear,* Edmund says Edgar arrives right on cue, like 'the catastrophe [the complication] of the old comedy' (1.3.136).

What do references like this do? Are they teaching the audience how to read genre or responding to the audience's preconceptions or satirizing generic assumptions or foregrounding Hope's and Witmore's 'generic oscillation' or …?

(Un)fashionable language

I began this chapter by looking at genre in relation to the plot of *Othello* (elopement), character (the Vice figure) and atmosphere (epic, heroic) before considering potential lexical

indications of genre – 'gull', 'is't possible?', 'no remedy'.
Language in *Othello* takes us back to genre – or genre takes
us back to language – in other ways too.

When Othello says his sexual faculties are 'defunct'
(1.3.265), one recalls that this was one of the new-fangled
words used by John Marston and ridiculed by Ben Jonson
when he stages (and parodies) Marston (under the name
Crispinus) in *Poetaster* (1601). In a comically climactic scene
the character Horace administers an emetic to make Crispinus
vomit up his outlandish vocabulary.

> *Crispinus.* Oh, I am sick.
> *Horace.*   A basin, a basin, quickly; our physic works.
>   Faint not, man.
> [*Horace holds a basin into which Crispinus appears to
>   vomit his words*]
> *Crispinus.* Oh – *retrograde* – *reciprocal* – *incubus.*
> *Caesar.*   What's that, Horace?
> *Horace.*   *Retrograde*, *reciprocal*, and *incubus* are come
>   up.
> *Gallus.*   Thanks be to Jupiter.
> *Crispinus.* Oh – *glibbery* – *lubrical* – *defunct* – Oh –
> *Horace.*   Well said; here's some store!
>
> (5.3.425)

Poetaster was staged in 1601. Just a year or more later,
Shakespeare bravely recuperates the word, claiming for it
the exoticism of Othello's vocabulary elsewhere in the play.
Othello's '[e]clipse' (5.2.98) and 'extenuate' (5.2.340) feature
in Robert Cawdrey's *Table Alphabetical … of Hard Usual
English Words* [i.e. a Dictionary] (1604), as does Roderigo's
'extravagant' (1.1.134) and Cassio's 'extincted' (2.1.81, where
Cawdrey's entry is for 'extinct'). As it happens, 'defunct'
appears nowhere in the works of John Marston.

Bawdy courts

But genre is also about narrative – not just the stories one tells but the way one tells them (as we saw in Chapter 1, when Othello presents his heroic epic identity to Desdemona, an identity he tries to recuperate in Act Five). This is as true of individuals as it is of plays. Iago's narrative strategy (one among many) is to take the play's story from the world of military heroism to the world (and language) of the bawdy courts.

'Bawdy court' is a colloquial, not an official, term for consistory or ecclesiastical courts: ad hoc hearings, held in church, presided over by the vicar (and churchwardens) in which members of the community lodged complaints about matters of reputation: slander, scandal, adultery, incest, prostitution, vituperation … Cases were tried in the hours before the Sunday service (Jonathan Bate likens them to the gossip sections of our Sunday newspapers) and the term 'bawdy court' summarizes these courts' most frequent and pruriently titillating subjects.

To accuse a woman of being a whore need not mean that the accuser actually thought the woman was promiscuous. It was 'the most readily available form of assault on a woman's reputation' (Jardine, 25) and in the York records, '90% of cases concerning a female plaintiff involved her sexual reputation' (Jardine, 26). 'Whore' is thus less a category than a general insult; the word is detached from its meaning. Detaching words from meaning is Iago's habit and so it is little wonder that he adopts this already-detached category with relish and ease. Iago's private scurrilities about Desdemona, as he comments on the way Cassio 'takes her by the palm' in Act Two, become public defamation as Othello first slaps and accuses Desdemona in public (4.1) and then brings her to trial in the bedchamber, where she dies 'in a state of undress – a whore's death' (Jardine, 31).

Jonathan Bate offers further parallels between the bawdy court and *Othello*. 'In the bawdy court cases, it is usually women who spread gossip, sexual insult and slander. In *Othello*, it is Iago who plays this role. The bawdy court was the testing-place of woman's "reputation". In *Othello*, it is Iago who destroys reputation by acting as a malicious bawd' (Bate, 47).

In the context of the bawdy courts, a key word in *Othello* assumes another significance: occupation. As Bate explains, the 'verb "occupy" frequently occurs in sex cases, as when one Isabel South accused Richard Todd in the following terms: "thou art a whoremaster and thou didst offer to give me an angel of gold to occupy me and thou didst offer another man's wife the making of an oven to occupy her"'. Bate notes: 'When Othello laments that his "occupation" is gone, he is referring not only to his military career but also to his sexual possession of Desdemona' (Bate, 47). The vocabulary, like the play itself, moves from the heroic world to the domestic.

And in this domestic world all three women are called whores. The more knowing Emilia and Bianca instantly defend themselves. In 5.1, Bianca says 'I am no strumpet, / But of life as honest as you, that thus / Abuse me' (5.1.121–2). Emilia likewise counters Iago – 'some such squire he was / That turned your wit the seamy side without / And made you to suspect me with the Moor (4.2.147–9 cf. Iago at 1.3.385–7, 2.1.293–4). Both Emilia and Bianca, as Lisa Jardine points out, recognize the need to overturn their defamation but the innocent Desdemona cannot even say the word 'whore'. She does not recognize the genre she is in. Instead of countering her accusation and treatment, she tries to rationalize it. Perhaps, she reasons, Othello suspects that her father is behind his recall to Venice and blames Desdemona for this:

> If haply you my father do suspect
> An instrument of this your calling back,
> Lay not your blame on me.

(4.2.45–7)

She ponders the meaning of the accusation: 'Am I that name? … I am sure I am none such' (4.2.120, 125).

Generically *Othello* is unusual among Shakespeare tragedies in being a domestic tragedy – that subgenre of tragedy, set in non-aristocratic or non-noble households, in which domestic violence impacts on the larger community. (Other contemporary examples include the anonymous *Arden of Faversham* (1594), based on a real crime committed in Kent in the 1550s, the anonymous *A Warning for Fair Women* (1599), and Thomas Heywood's *A Woman Killed with Kindness* (1603).) But *Othello* is more than just a Shakespearean variant or contribution: one of Iago's generic triumphs is to reduce the heroic to the domestic and then further reduce it to the petty, slandering, defamatory, salacious – linguistic – world of the bawdy court.

Tragedy without Shakespeare's language

We have been exploring genre in this chapter, and genre's relation to language. I want, in these final sections, to consider how *Othello* works as a tragedy when it lacks Shakespeare's language. We will look at a Caroline stage adaptation by John Ford before moving to twentieth-century film adaptations for television and cinema.

John Ford

In the 1620s the playwright John Ford dramatically rewrote the *Othello* story in a tragedy called *Love's Sacrifice*. (*Love's Sacrifice* could well be the title of Shakespeare's play, given that Othello tells Desdemona 'thou … makest me call what I intend to do / A murder, which I thought a sacrifice';

5.2.63–5.) Ford's play was written between 1621 and 1633 (probably, more specifically, between 1626 and 1631; Moore ed., *Love's Sacrifice*, 2). Shakespeare's *Othello* remained a popular play on stage in the 1620s. Performances of *Othello* are recorded at the Blackfriars Theatre as late as 1629. Thus *Love's Sacrifice* is not only in dialogue with *Othello* but in the London repertory with it: it was performed at the Phoenix indoor theatre from c. 1626 to 1639.

In *Love's Sacrifice* we have an Othello figure, the Duke of Pavy; a Desdemona figure, his young bride, Bianca; an Iago figure, the Duke's secretary, D'Avolos; and a Cassio figure, the Duke's close friend, the young nobleman Fernando. The Duke is keen for Fernando to meet and warm to Bianca. Fernando immediately falls in love but Bianca resists his overtures; later she reveals that she loves him and although they kiss, they do not consummate their passion.

Bianca is not as white as her name suggests and the play introduces ambiguities that are unthinkable in *Othello*. In 2.1 Bianca chastely rebuffs Fernando's advances:

> It is the third time since your treacherous tongue
> Hath pleaded treason to my ear and fame;
> Yet for the friendship 'twixt my lord and you,
> I have not voiced your follies. If you dare
> To speak a fourth time, you shall rue your lust.
> 'Tis all no better: learn and love yourself.

> (2.1.141–6)

Fernando tells us: 'I have sued and sued, / Kneeled, wept and begged; but tears, and vows, and words / Move her no more than summer winds a rock' (2.1.150–3). The exchange is reinforced by its repetition in 2.3 (this time the scene is overlooked and misinterpreted by D'Avolos). Yet in 2.4 Bianca enters Fernando's bedchamber in her nightgown and confesses she has loved him from first sight; she offers him her body and invites him to 'ruin' her (2.4.48). Although the

couple kiss, they go no further which is why, when the Duke
and Fernando fight after Bianca's death in Act Five, Fernando
can defend Bianca's reputation:

> Thou hast butchered
> An innocent, a wife as free from lust
> As any terms of art can deify.

(5.2.53–5)

However, before she dies, Bianca gives the Duke a tongue-
lashing description of his elderly lack of erotic appeal when
compared to the youthful beauties of Fernando (5.1.72–82;
95–103). The bewildered Duke muses, 'I matched [married]
a woman, but I find she is / A devil worser than the worst in
hell' (5.1.110–11). Even so, at her funeral, her husband and
her lover talk of her as a martyr.

The creation of this non-Desdemona-like Bianca is a
perplexing change in a plot that otherwise references *Othello*
closely. Goaded to suspicion by D'Avolos, the Duke delivers a
speech indebted to Othello's Pontic Sea lines:

> The icy current of my frozen blood
> Is kindled up in agonies as hot
> As flames of burning sulphur. O my fate!
> A cuckold? Had my dukedom's whole inheritance
> Been rent, mine honours levelled in the dust,
> So she, that wicked woman, might have slept
> Chaste in my bosom, 't had been all a sport.
> And he, that villain, viper to my heart,
> That he should be the man! ...
> Take heed you prove this true.

(3.3.57–67)

Fernando and the Duke's sister have a conversation about
the Duke's unusual jealousy, a jealousy which has 'no cause'
(4.1.23.4). And D'Avolos, in plot and language, repeatedly

references his Shakespearean predecessor. In Act Three, Fernando and Bianca converse in the presence of the Duke and D'Avolos:

> *D'Avolos.* Beshrew my heart, but that's not so good.
> *Duke.* Ha! What's that thou mislik'st, D'Avolos?
> *D'Avolos.* Nothing, my lord.
> …
> *D'Avolos.* A shrewd ominous token; I like not that neither.
> *Duke.* Again! What is't you like not?
>
> (3.2.50–2, 68–9)

The Duke later confronts D'Avolos more directly than Othello ever does Iago, but with the same aim: to resolve doubt. He summarizes d'Avolos' tactics – the tactics we have seen on stage, both in the previous scene and in Shakespeare's earlier play:

> Did not I note your dark abrupted ends
> Of words half-spoke? Your 'wells, if all were known'?
> Your short 'I like not that?' Your girds [gibes] and 'buts'?
> Yes sir, I did. Such broken language argues
> More matter than your subtlety shall hide.
> Tell me, what is't? By honour's self, I'll know.
>
> (3.3.5–10)

D'Avolos protests his ignorance and says he will not invent things: 'Should I devise matter to feed your distrust, or suggest likelihoods without appearance?' (3.3.13–15). (Feeding distrust and suggesting likelihoods without appearance are, of course, precisely his and Iago's tactics.)

In the denouement (the resolution and untangling of a plot – literally, an unknotting) of 5.2, the Duke, like Othello, identifies D'Avolos as a devil:

Note him, my lords.
If you would choose a devil in the shape
Of man, an arch-arch-devil, there stands one.

(5.2.103–5)

D'Avolos is sanguine: '"Arch-arch-devil"? Why, I am paid. Here's bounty for good service'. He hopes to be let off but after the next scene has completed the play's tragic ending (the Duke commits suicide after a speech that, like Othello's, moves from the first- to the third-person), the new ruler commands that D'Avolos be hanged alive. D'Avolos, unlike Iago, is given a shoulder-shrugging exit line: 'Here's my comfort: I make but one in the number of the tragedy of princes' (5.3.150–1).

Unlike *Othello*, which has a single-strand plot in Iago's deception of Othello, *Love's Sacrifice* has several subsidiary strands. The Duke's romance is paralleled and parodied in the story of an amorous old courtier, Mauriccio. Another courtier, a wanton young man, Ferentes, manages to get not one but three women pregnant and they succeed in killing him at the end of Act Three. Fernando, the Cassio character who loves Bianca, is himself loved by the Duke's widowed sister, Fiormonda; and she is served by a fool, who happens to be a banished nobleman in disguise, who is in love with her. Fiormonda's role is important in motivating D'Avolos: he is in Fiormonda's employ and confidence. She entices him to facilitate her romance with Fernando ('Prevail, and I will raise thee high in grace'; 1.1.199). When Fernando proves unreceptive, D'Avolos suspects he loves elsewhere and this prompts him to bring down Bianca.

Let us be clear about what Ford adopts and adapts from Shakespeare. He takes Othello's language and his jealousy; he takes Iago's villainy and his linguistic tactics. The implicit comedy of *Othello* he makes explicit by introducing comic plots and characters: Mauriccio is a pantaloon and Ferentes is a Mercutio-character (Mercutio is Romeo's comic friend in *Romeo and Juliet*) whose early death aligns the play's structure more with *Romeo and Juliet* than with *Othello*. (*Romeo and Juliet* is referenced again in the romantic competition between Fernando and the Duke in Act Five and the former's suicide by poison.) Ford adds motivation for D'Avolos and removes the cryptic soliloquizing relationship Iago enjoys with the audience. And he turns Desdemona/ Bianca from white into grey. All the changes can be easily explained except this last.

We may approach this puzzle by returning to the middle of the three scenes that Bianca shares with Fernando. In the first she rebuffs him, in the third she offers herself to him; in the second the couple are overheard or overseen by D'Avolos. In this middle scene Bianca unequivocally, and for a second time on stage, rejects Fernando. He now accepts his rejection, vowing never to approach her again. To cement this vow he kisses her hand.

But D'Avolos misinterprets this scene. In the first of his three short comments he laments that the amorous action is too slow and that Fernando kneels chivalrously rather than leaping into bed (3.2.64–7). In the second, he interprets Bianca's long rejection speech as encouragement (3.2.88). In the third, when Fernando kisses Bianca's hand, D'Avolos concludes, 'Ay, marry, the match is made, clap hands and to't, ho!' He then summarizes the action to Fiormonda: 'I saw him kneel, make pitiful faces, kiss hands and forefingers, rise, and by this time he is up, up, madam. Doubtless the youth aims to be Duke, for he is gotten into the Duke's seat an hour ago' (2.3.117–21).

Iago too observes Cassio take Desdemona 'by the palm' and kiss his own fingers (presumably to send kisses as he does in the 1964 National Theatre production). Roderigo rightly interprets this as 'courtesy'; Iago deliberately misunderstands this as 'lechery' (*Othello* 2.1.167, 254–5). But in Ford, D'Avolos' misunderstanding seems not to be manipulative but genuine.

Critics note that *Love's Sacrifice* is a play about interpretation: the play's emphasis on 'social knowledge and feeling which count as true representations of others or oneself' has the effect of 'bringing all signifying behaviours, whether visual or verbal, under scrutiny' (Moore ed. *Love's Sacrifice*, 27). A. T. Moore is surely right to attribute this to the influence of *Othello*, a play which, as we have seen, repeatedly foregrounds multiple and contradictory interpretations whether of objects (Ottoman ships, a handkerchief) or humans or genres. D'Avolos' interpretation of the scene between Bianca and Fernando is so different from what we have seen that it forces us to rethink what we (thought we) saw:

> Was D'Avolos mistaken in his cynicism and only 'made right', in retrospect by a real change in Bianca? Or did D'Avolos see (or hear) something that we, in our naivety, did not?
>
> (Moore ed. *Love's Sacrifice*, 27)

The questions are unanswerable. But the fact that the play forces us to ask them shows Ford actively engaging with the epistemological problems that *Othello* poses. As Moore says, we get an 'impression of Ford meditating on his principal source rather than simply capitalizing on its theatrical potential' (Moore ed. *Love's Sacrifice,* 27).

Of particular interest here is the way in which Moore, en passant, links this indeterminate scene to genre:

> D'Avolos' version differs so wildly from the apparent truth that the villain's seeming misconstructions *could easily be played as comedy.*
>
> (Moore ed. *Love's Sacrifice*, 27, my italics)

The scene's generic indeterminacy may be part of the play's interest in epistemological indeterminacy.

So too is the splicing together of Shakespeare sources. *Othello* and *Romeo and Juliet* are the two Shakespeare tragedies that begin as comedies. The two Shakespeare tragedies that begin as comedy caught Ford's eye and his ear. Taken together they offer Ford two different romantic models. In *Romeo and Juliet* the lovers are sacrifices to an 'ancient grudge', victims of a family feud, 'romantic rebels' manipulated by fate (Moore ed. *Love's Sacrifice*, 30). In *Othello* the manipulations are those of Iago: it is he who betrays Othello, not Desdemona. Ford combines these two plays. He complicates the questions about interpretation and evidence, partly by staging them generically (is Act 3, scene 2 comic or serious?). But in expanding the plot to include a host of sub-characters and additional comic actions, he also dilutes what is, for me, one of *Othello*'s special characteristics: its intensity. *Othello* is unusual among Shakespeare's tragedies in its unidirectional concentration, its single plot about the unravelling of a marriage.

Modernizing *Othello*

Let us move now to two modern film adaptations – the teen movie O (2001, directed by Tim Blake Nelson) where Othello's military achievements and service to the state are relocated to the world of high school basketball, and a British TV adaptation, *Othello* (2001, written by Andrew Davies and directed by Geoffrey Sax), where John Othello becomes the first black Commissioner of the London Metropolitan Police Force. Like Ford's *Love's Sacrifice* these versions take the plot or the character of *Othello* and offer us tragedy without the hallmarks of Shakespeare's language.

Michael Neill begs to differ, however, and sees 'tragedy' as too grand a term for either of the film adaptations, calling O 'unrelievedly pedestrian' adding that 'little more can be said for Andrew Davies' television play, *Othello*, misleadingly subtitled "A Modern Masterpiece"', and accusing it of 'banality' (Neill ed. *Othello*, 7). It is worth unpacking these accusations.

Certainly, the tragic power of *Othello* has long been associated with its language. George Bernard Shaw found *Othello* splendid because of its

> word-music, which sweeps the scenes up to a plane on which sense is drowned in sound. The words do not convey ideas: they are streaming ensigns and tossing branches to make the tempest of passion visible ... Tested by the brain, it is ridiculous: tested by the ear, it is sublime.
> (Wilson, 171–2) (Incidentally, Shaw was not consistent in this view. See Neill ed. *Othello*, 6 n.1)

The logical corollary of this is that if one removes the sublimity of the ear's experience, we are left with the brain's experience: the plot is ridiculous. (Remember Thomas Rymer: 'never was any play fraught, like this of Othello, with improbabilities'; 'the Fable [is] ... absurd'; Rymer, 134.)

We should note, however, that Shaw's view here of the 'passion' of the language, and G. Wilson Knight's later, famous, identification of the Othello music, apply only to one character in the play – the protagonist, Othello. Othello's dramatic power is located in rhetoric, in cosmic images, in mouth-filling words. Iago's is not. But that is not to say his power is not linguistic. His low cunning, his improvisatory wit, his dialogue with the audience, his manipulation of language is prosaic (in a literal sense) and may transfer very well to the world of modern prose and the television screen.

Although Shakespeare adaptations are often spectacularly artistically successful – *West Side Story* (musical 1957, film 1961), *Forbidden Planet* (1956), *Ten Things I Hate About You* (1999) – critical anxiety and negative comment focuses on (the loss of) language. Analysing O, Alexander Leggatt writes

> The power of his [Othello's] last speech is ... reduced from the original. While Othello in his last moments commands

eloquence, Odin's equivalent speech is broken, distraught, slurred.

(Leggatt 2006, 256)

Lisa Hopkins complains that 'the closing sequences [of Davies' *Othello*] develop very differently from in Shakespeare, and not just because Davies has so thoroughly jettisoned the play's language' (Hopkins 2002, §4). Daniel Rosenthal acknowledges that theatre directors have long appreciated the value of modernizing an Elizabethan text, but only in the rehearsal room where paraphrase is used to help the actor find the emotion in the Shakespearean line. Rosenthal gives an example of a modern paraphrase of four lines of *Othello* before concluding:

> multiply this example by a couple of hundred and you realise why even superb modern adaptations such as the LWT [London Weekend Television: the company that commissioned and broadcast Davies' *Othello*] will always rank as Shakespeare lite.

(Rosenthal, 7)

Shakespeare lite, perhaps, but not tragedy lite: both these adaptations show the play's gut-wrenching pain even without the 'Othello music'.

Othello (adapted by Andrew Davies, 2001)

The 1990s police force setting of Davies' adaptation had an urgent British topicality in the wake of the Stephen Lawrence inquiry. Stephen Lawrence was a black teenager from London who was murdered in a racially motivated attack while waiting for a bus in 1993. The inquiry into his death also investigated the London Metropolitan Police Force and found them guilty of institutional racism.

The film begins with a raid on a black drug suspect by four police officers who beat the suspect to death. John Othello steps forward (like Shakespeare's Thomas More reasoning with the xenophobic crowd in the manuscript history play, *Sir Thomas More*) to calm the subsequent race riots, promising that 'if Billy Coates was unlawfully killed, there will be no place for his killer to hide. We must have justice, justice under the law.' The resignation of the police Commissioner propels Othello into the limelight, to the anger and resentment of Ben Jago, who had been groomed as the Commissioner's replacement. The media coverage of Othello and his newly-wed white wife Dessie make Dessie vulnerable and so she is placed under police guard – that of Superintendent Michael Cass.

The domestic tragedy emerges late in the film; the first half focuses on the professional issues. The internal police investigation that follows Billy Coates's death gives us the contradictory accounts that characterize Shakespeare's play. The scenes we see in the film's opening are of a threatening suspect and an accidental death. The four police officers remain united in their subsequent story, repeating it in identical official language ('I feared for my life'; 'we used only approved methods'). When the junior constable finally tells the truth (there was no weapon; the suspect was merely sexually provocative, flaunting not a knife but his penis; one of the police constables 'just lost it'), the film then screens the events in flashback, not as first shown but in the corrected version.

Nonetheless this resolution does not lead to a happy ending. The truthful young constable, Alan Roderick (a professionally idealistic Roderigo figure who witnessed but did not participate in Coates's killing) commits suicide under the pressure of the punitive hostility to him by his 'betrayed' colleagues. Here we have a betrayer in a professional sphere who is full of integrity (he says he couldn't live with himself if he concealed the truth) and of personal anguish (the camera chronicles his torments and tears as he vacillates between truth and apparent betrayal) but whose plot leads to tragedy.

When, during the police inquiry, Jago says 'There might just be a happy ending to this after all', it is hard to know whether he is being ironic.

The plot's other betrayer, Ben Jago, has, as in Shakespeare's play, no integrity or internal agony; but unlike Shakespeare's play, he triumphs. Jago succeeds Othello professionally in the Met. This has been his desideratum from the start of the film where the opening sequences splice shots of the raid on Billy Coates with scenes at the annual Metropolitan Police black-tie dinner; the Commissioner, Sinclair Carver, is announcing a policy to increase the number of ethnic officers 'at the highest level'. Carver's public stance of inclusivity is belied by the racist views he voices to Jago in the privacy of the urinal, remarks that, overheard and leaked, force his resignation. (I resist the temptation to speculate about Davies' visual pun on 'leaks' in this scene.) The overhearer is not a journalist but a senior police officer. It's OK, reasons Carver to Jago as they assess the potential damage: 'he's one of us'. The film thus introduces its first betrayal within the ranks, a betrayal which is, like Roderick's, in the public interest.

As Assistant Commissioner, Jago is Carver's right-hand man. But the friendship is not as reciprocal as it appears. Jago has a confessional relationship with the viewer through direct address to the camera and tells us that Carver is 'yesterday's man'. This is before Carver makes the racist remarks that force his resignation.

The film has a series of head and shoulders close-ups of male characters hugging. The first comes at the start of Carver's downfall with the press camped outside his door. Jago assures Carver of his allegiance: 'I am your man – always have been, always will be'. Jago looks knowingly at us over Carver's shoulder, ironizing his statement of allegiance. He later hugs Roderick when emotionally persuading the distressed young constable to shop his colleagues. When Othello is promoted to the position of Chief Commissioner, he hugs Jago and the camera shows the emotions in Othello's face as he relaxes into

Jago's shoulder. 'I'm so proud of you', says Jago, gritting his teeth while looking directly at us.

Jago later re-enacts the dialogue in this scene, replaying Othello's expressions of gratitude but this time adding Jago's previously unspoken responses (for example, 'you stupid black ape'). As he storms up and down a corridor, we see his venom. So does he: in the next shot he comments to us on his loss of control – 'Well, well, what a performance. It's going to take longer than I hoped. It'll end in broken hearts. Not yours or mine' – before telling us, 'Cheer up'.

Jago's relationship with the camera, like Iago's soliloquizing to the audience, provides much of the film's propulsion and power. Even when not talking directly to us, Jago is constantly aware of us: he looks over his shoulder to the camera, he holds up newspaper headlines for us to read. Lisa Hopkins confesses that from early in the film she was 'completely in thrall to Christopher Eccleston's Ben Jago' because of 'the way he flirts with the camera' (Hopkins, §1).

Jago's words to the camera are not the opaque soliloquizing of Iago. They are explanations, revelations of his motive. 'It was about love; that's what you've got to understand. Don't talk to me about race. Don't talk to me about politics. It was love, simple as that'; 'I loved him too'. This voiceover begins the film and it is repeated at the end. Late in the film, after an ugly scene in a restaurant (Davies' equivalent of the humiliation of Desdemona in 4.1), Jago asks for our opinion: 'So, what do you think?' Clearly guessing our response, he replies, 'I know. I feel it. I'm almost sorry I started this. Too late now. It's up and running. It's beyond my control.' (His terms here echo those of Anouilh, quoted at the start of this chapter.) Later he offers a variant of this to Othello, apologetically, after Dessie's death, saying that 'he never meant it to end like this'. One is almost inclined to believe him. At the start of the film he tells us, in a proleptic retrospective of the action we are about to watch, 'Tragedy, right. No other word for it' – a tantalizing suggestion that the genre was not the one he had anticipated (*prolepsis* is an anticipation of something). But moments like this are undercut by scenes such as the one in which he recommends Michael Cass as bodyguard for Dessie. He tells Othello that Dessie needs 'someone she can talk to. Someone she can be easy with'. He then looks at us interrogatively, as if to say, 'And what's he then that says I play the villain? / When this advice is free I give and honest' (2.3.331–2).

As in many stage productions, Jago is a mimic and ventriloquist. Reading newspaper interviews with Dessie about her husband's promotion, he turns the headline into a simpering, 'I feel so safe with him'. In his head he replays Othello's heartfelt comments of gratitude, inflecting them with patronizing condescension. Playing erotically in the bath with his new girlfriend, Lulu (Dessie's best friend) he asks if she'd prefer to go jogging, imitating an imagined conversation between Othello and Dessie.

Jago's transformation of Othello into a suspicious and murderous husband is done, as in Shakespeare, with subtle linguistic economy. Michael Cass, he suggests, 'is enjoying his work a bit too much'. Press photos of Cass accompanying Dessie on her jogs '*could* be quite innocent'. He concludes a conversation with 'Good. Nothing to worry about then. Probably', where the optative adverb 'probably' undoes the prior confidence. Like Iago, Jago is a master of the psychology of negation: 'And Dessie: you can tell she's put her wild times behind her'. Here the split meanings are aimed at Othello (Othello hears not the reassurance ostensibly offered but its opposite: 'maybe she *hasn't* put her wild times behind her'). At other times they are aimed at us and Othello is deaf to them. 'Sir' is said in inverted commas; Othello hears deference, we hear the way his rank rankles with Jago. When Othello and Jago are in conversation about the revelation of police racism and brutality, the two talk at cross purposes: Othello sees the outcome as the result of his determination, Jago as a result of his skill. When Othello finally compliments Jago on his ability, Jago's reply is full of jocular exaggeration that he pitches to Othello as playful but which we hear as sarcasm: 'Thank you John. Your saying that makes it all worthwhile'.

The film occasionally references Shakespearean language or paraphrases specific speeches. Asked what she was like before she met him, Dessie tells Othello she was 'like a blank sheet waiting for you to write your name upon me'. Iago's description of the will as a garden in which we sow what we like is transferred to Jago's description of women's bodies as a secret sexual garden. Like Shakespeare's Iago, Jago tells the truth: 'I'm just a suspicious bastard', he tells Othello. Othello tells Dessie that 'I think I love you too much'. When Jago finds not just Dessie but Othello 'too good to be true', we are reminded of the 'daily beauty' Iago observes in Shakespeare's Cassio's life. We see Othello's rhetorical ability when he placates the rioting crowd, and in the frequent references to his courtship of Dessie as one in which he 'did all the talking and [she] did all the listening'. Othello's accusation of Dessie as a 'bitch' and a 'whore' is so linguistically brutal in the film after the couple's verbal tenderness that the terms work as the single word 'whore' does in *Othello*, as a violent acoustic assault on us, the audience, as well as on the innocent wife.

Other Shakespearean references are conveyed visually. Othello's exotic origins are evident in an elegant Moroccan-themed apartment and a scene in a Moroccan restaurant. Official photographs of Othello for his new post have the exoticism of the portrait of Elizabeth I's Moorish Ambassador, not because of his blackness but because of his official Commissioner's dress, complete with white-plumed helmet. A different kind of domestic textile replaces the handkerchief as the sexually symbolic item. It is a gift not from Othello to Desdemona but from her to him: a sumptuous silk dressing-gown (worn first by Desdemona and, once, when red wine is spilled on his white shirt, incriminatingly by Michael Cass). The scene in the hotel's urinal is the first of several overhearing scenes, where, unlike *Othello*, the content is correctly understood. (Othello audits the internal police inquiry from an adjacent booth.)

The film departs from the play in two major ways. Cass gets drunk on champagne when celebrating his birthday and clumsily makes a pass at Dessie (which she rejects, firmly redrawing the professional boundaries). He has been encouraged to make this move by Jago's suggestion that Dessie is attracted to him and that her marriage to Othello is 'a show marriage'. Jago's goading of Othello with mendacious suggestions about Dessie's infidelity culminates not in a further manipulation of language or imagination but in a factual lie: he says DNA evidence on Othello's dressing-gown proves Cass had sex with Dessie. These two items remove the subtlety of the psychological torture in Shakespeare's play and negate its interest in Othello's capacity for imaginative extension of inferences. But the DNA also provides Jago with an escape route: in the end he is able to claim that 'they cocked up at the lab. She's innocent, John. She's clean'. This is very different from Iago's 'I told him what I thought, and told no more / Than what he found himself was apt and true' (5.2.172–3) or his later refusal to say anything in defence of himself ('What you know, you know'; 5.2.300). Lulu, however, is not convinced and, unlike her counterpart, Emilia, she ends the film alive; one wonders, hopefully, about her capacity to investigate and unravel events, as she does in the play's source story in Cinthio.

Part of the film's tragic power comes from its sequential stacking of 'if only' moments. If one definition of tragedy is that 'it did not need to be this way', this adaptation shares with the play a number of moments when things might have been other than they turn out. This power comes from structure not from language. Davies' Metropolitan Police setting enables him to add an extra element to this kind of knife-twisting because, as Hopkins realizes, it looks like Othello might actually be able to solve the problems of racism in the Metropolitan Police. It is, she says, 'his eventual failure to do so [that] makes the end doubly distressing' (Hopkins, §3). Here, comedic evitability comes up against tragic inevitability.

In the film Jago works against Othello in two directions simultaneously, domestically and professionally. The domestic comes from Shakespeare's play; the professional comes from the political setting in the police force at a time of racial crisis. Jago presents Roderick's suicide to the Home Office as the consequence of Othello's pressurizing him to 'put a spin on his story' in order to secure a conviction; and he hints that Othello is not coping with the pressure ('We're looking after him as best we can'). The film ends with a glib dialogue between Home Office politicians: the promotion of Othello has been 'an interesting experiment'; the black professional was given 'too much too soon'; and his private life is reduced to 'woman troubles'. What is needed now is a 'safe pair of hands' – Ben Jago.

Othello's 'woman' troubles were, in fact, 'man' troubles. My gender substitute in this conventional phrase about romantic difficulties indicates the film's queer sub text (at times not so 'sub'). The voiceovers in which Jago says that he was motivated by love bookend the film. Combined with the shots of Jago hugging men – and although there are three such shots, the common denominator in them is Jago – they give the film a gay motivation. It may be relevant that Jago has two ex-wives and his new sexual relationship with Lulu is based on rutting rather than love. (When Antony Sher played Iago he noted that 'animals crop up a lot in his dirty talk' and he sees sex 'as a savage business ... there's certainly nothing loving about it'; Sher 66). Lulu realizes that Jago's interest in her may be more a desire to parallel Othello ('a posh girlfriend') than a desire for her. Gay explanations for Iago's behaviour are not infrequent on stage and in criticism (they colour Honigmann's introduction to his edition, for instance) although they are problematically offensive: gay men do not usually go around destroying heterosexual couples.

In this adaptation about 'man troubles', the man who caused the trouble inherits – the final image is of Jago posing for portraits in his new Commissioner's uniform. Jago's promotion makes this a domestic and a political tragedy with no cathartic quality to console us. Carver was a racist; Jago is also a racist (we see him agreeing with Carver in private and

talking about Othello in racist terms in a voiceover). Nothing
has changed.

O (directed by Tim Blake Nelson, 2001)

In O's transposed setting, the American boarding school
Palmetto Grove, Odin is the only black student on the
basketball team. His girlfriend, Desi, is the Dean's daughter.
The Roderigo character, Roger, is the son of a major donor;
and the Iago figure, Hugo, has a father, Duke, the basketball
coach who treats and loves Odin as if he were his own son.
He declares this sentiment in public when Odin wins the
MVP (Most Valuable Player) award which he spontaneously
chooses to share with Michael Cassio, inviting him onto the
stage to share the limelight. Hugo thus feels doubly excluded.
At the awards ceremony, Odin pays tribute to his 'go to guy'
and a close-up of Hugo makes it obvious that Hugo thinks
this will be him. Late in the film, Hugo accepts an invitation
from his father to dinner, with evident pleasure: 'it's been a
while since you invited me in for dinner'. Duke immediately
makes it clear that the meal has an agenda and that the agenda
is not father/son bonding: 'What's going on with Odin?' When
Hugo mentions that he is 'getting an A in English again', his
father is complacent about the achievement: 'You're doing
OK. Odin is different. Odin is the only black student in the
whole damn place. We're his family'. And so the film moves
towards a Columbine-style conclusion. (In fact, although the
film was released in 2001, the same year as *Othello* above,
it was shot in 1999, the year of the Columbine high school
massacre, and its release delayed.) Hugo is given an honest
interiority, and his relation to his father parallels Kevin's
with his mother in Lionel Shriver's novel *We Need to Talk
about Kevin* (2005). The film asks the same questions that
high school massacres (whether real or fictional) prompt: how
could a nice kid do this? In adding the role of Hugo's father,

it offers a clear if formulaic answer. At the end, Odin realizes how his story will be interpreted as racially stereotypical and he protests, 'My mom ain't no crackhead. He twisted my head off. I'm no different from any of you. It was this white prep school motherfucker fucked me off'.

Like Davies' *Othello*, Nelson's *O* begins and ends with a voiceover by the Iago character, Hugo: 'All my life I wanted to fly'. As in Davies' *Othello*, the repetition at the end clarifies the initial context. Here, the basketball team, with its hawk mascot and the identification of the star player, Odin, with a soaring matchless bird, explains Hugo's envy, as he himself makes clear in his end-of-film extension of his opening line: 'A hawk is no good around normal birds. It can't fit in. Other birds hate him for what they can't be'. Thus, the film ends with the Iago-figure's attempt to explain his life rather than the Othello-figure's.

In between these two moments, however, the film stays much closer to Shakespeare's text. Desi's father tells Odin, 'She deceived me' (cf. 1.3.294). Desi tells Odin, 'You do have the best stories' (cf. 1.3.146–7). Hugo says 'sometimes I see things that aren't really there' (3.3.150–2) and tells Odin 'I know white girls better than you' (3.3.204–6). Odin tells Hugo he can't deal with uncertainty (3.3.182–3). His narrative of the family importance of the silk scarf he gave Desi parallels Shakespeare's (3.4.58–65). Roger, set up as a pawn by Hugo, asks for clarification about what exactly has been achieved, like Shakespeare's Roderigo: 'Just for the record: why am I doing this again?' (2.3.358–64). Hugo's suggestions to Odin about Desdemona's two-timing are extended paraphrases of Shakespeare: 'If there is something going on with Mike – and I'm not saying there is –'; 'Watch her: if she hangs out with Mike, keeps talking about Mike, then we got something to talk about' (3.3.199–200). Hugo's girlfriend, Brandy, offers him Desi's scarf with the line 'I have something for you'; Hugo responds contemptuously, 'You've got things for lots of guys' (3.3.305–6). Hugo tells Odin, 'You're not a jealous person. I am' (3.3.150). And at the end, although Hugo's voiceover

offers an explanation to us, he says to the other characters,
'Ask me nothing. I did what I did and that's all you need to
know' (5.2.300–1).

Providing Hugo with a visible motive does not lessen the
painful focus on Odin and Desi. If anything, it increases it
because the audience has no privileged relationship with
Hugo, unable to be comically breathtaken by the audacity of a
Vice-figure. In the film, it is Othello who is the ludic figure. He
offers Desi a fake narrative of a scar on his back (a C-section
bungled by a cheap doctor who cut too deep) before the comic
bathos of the truth: a skateboarding accident.

Given that this is a teen movie, the teenage sex is chaste –
cuddling not penetration. When Desi later encourages Odin
to go further, it is after Hugo has convinced him that Desi
is seeing someone else. In the motel room mirror, Odin sees
not himself on top of Desi (who is protesting at his painful
sexual violence) but Mike Cassio. (So too Othello, going to
join Desdemona in bed in Oliver Parker's film, 'sees' her with
Cassio behind the white gauze bed curtains.)

Alexander Leggatt notes the film's images of entrapment:
school uniforms, bars in the gym, tall staircases, serried
trees in the school grounds, neoclassical pillars of the school
buildings (Leggatt 2006, 254). When the film juxtaposes
its own modern language with a modern paraphrase of a
Shakespearean line, the latter acts as a disciplinary generic
straitjacket, bringing back to Shakespeare's plot a character's
chance of escaping it. For Leggatt, the modern lines represent
the characters' bids for freedom before a Shakespeare line in
response pulls them back into Shakespeare's play, trapping
them in Shakespeare's dialogue (Leggatt 2006, 253). This
juxtaposition of two kinds of language thus works to curtail
Snyder's evitability and move it into tragic inevitability.
The sound track does the same: the Ave Maria from Verdi's
Otello punctuates the film, offering an additional generic
straitjacket. Hugo wants to 'soar' like a hawk, and at the
end, led handcuffed to a police car, says 'everyone is gonna
pay attention to me now because I'm going to fly now'. The

statement is ironized by Verdi's music: the only thing that soars is the score.

O adds two characters: a pharmacist who gives Hugo steroid injections (and advice) and a pawnbroker from whom Hugo acquires a .38 pistol in exchange for his watch. These characters reflect the influence of *Romeo and Juliet* (an influence we also saw in John Ford's Caroline stage adaptation of *Othello*). The pharmacist is a Friar Laurence figure (from *Romeo and Juliet*) who offers Hugo cautionary wisdom about drugs and life. For instance, he tells Hugo 'Some things in life we weren't meant to have', a sage counter to Hugo's voiceovers about hating Odin for what he is and Hugo can't be. The pawnbroker functions like the apothecary in *Romeo and Juliet* where he offers a fatal material (poison in *Romeo and Juliet*, the pistol in *O*) with great misgivings, transacting only because of financial need. 'My poverty, but not my will consents', says Shakespeare's Apothecary, receiving the curt rebuff from Romeo, 'I pay thy poverty and not thy will' (5.1.75–6). So too Hugo reassures the pawnbroker that the exchange does not violate moral law but fulfils two needs: 'You want that watch, I want that pistol'.

Whereas Davies' *Othello* stresses Jago's love for Othello, *O* stresses Hugo's hate: 'A hawk is no good round normal birds. It can't fit in. The other birds hate him for what they can't be'. Instead, love for Othello/Odin is redirected into paternal love: Duke says, 'I love him like my own son'. Despite this statement, Duke does not offer parity of paternal love, as we saw above in the dinner scene with Hugo and as we see again in a tense and silent family dinner Hugo has with both parents. When, in the first of Hugo's successful machinations against Odin, he stirs Odin into such an emotional frenzy that he behaves violently on the basketball court, Hugo says to us, 'Yeah, dad, who's your favourite now?'

The tragic end that Hugo engineers is complex: it involves careful timing, two cars, an automobile break down, a pistol, and the murder of Michael Cassio in a way that will look like suicide. (It goes wrong when Roger shoots Michael in the improbable suicide area of the leg and Hugo panics.) But as he is planning and stage-managing this climax, Hugo reassures Roger that nothing can go wrong: 'all we have to do is set things in motion and never look back'. Like Jago's comment in *Othello* above, this is very close to Anouilh's remark about tragedy at the start of this chapter: 'The spring is wound up tight. It will uncoil of itself'. Hugo knows how tragedy works and this is the genre he is self-consciously engineering.

So far I have been looking at these films for their generic interest – the ways in which they create Shakespearean tragedy despite their distance from Shakespeare's language and the ways in which their allusions to the source play create a knowing intertextual relationship. I want to pursue the issue of intertextuality. But first we need to bring another film to the discussion: Richard Eyre's *Stage Beauty* (2004).

Stage Beauty (directed by Richard Eyre, 2004)

The setting and context for Eyre's *Stage Beauty* are loosely historical, a Restoration London in which Ned Kynaston plays Shakespearean heroines – until Charles II changes the law, allowing women to act female parts. As Kynaston loses the limelight, his dresser, Maria, emerges as a successful Desdemona, despite her wooden copycat acting – she plays Kynaston playing Desdemona, reproducing his stereotyped gestures ('the five positions of feminine subjugation; the stamp of girlish petulance').

This is a film about genre and gender. (Indeed, the two are linked lexically as both come from the same Latin root, *genus*, meaning a kind of person or thing by birth, race, stock.) Kynaston is puzzled by the suggestion that women might play female roles ('a woman playing a woman – what's the trick in that?') or that he might play a man ('there is no artistry in that'). Maria just 'want[s] to act'. When Kynaston counters that he has spent 'half his life learning to do what I do', Maria (eventually) criticizes his performance. He has not learned 'to suffer like a woman'. His Desdemona 'dies beautifully'. No woman would die like that. A woman would fight'.

When Kynaston auditions for the role of Othello in front of Charles II, his cross-dressed, mannered, formulaic, highly artificial Desdemona-acting becomes laughable (literally: the scene is comic). Through its setting in a moment of theatrical transition, *Stage Beauty* portrays the extent to which genre is dependent on and defined by acting conventions.

Kynaston and Maria eventually discover twentieth-century Method acting (a school of training in which the actor strives to identify emotionally with the character); a rehearsal scene and a performance show their triumph in an anachronistically naturalistic *Othello*. Even Charles II who, at the start of the film had responded to *Othello* with the querulous 'Could you make it cheerier?', finds the 'new ending – restorative somehow'.

Gender switching is not confined to the theatre. Kynaston is the lover of George Villiers, Duke of Buckingham who tells him, 'I always thought of you as a woman'. When Kynaston loses his job, Buckingham says 'You're none of them [Desdemona / Cleopatra / Ophelia] now. I don't know who you are'. The lecherous Sir Charles Sedley sees Kynaston outside the theatre in his female stage costume and pursues him sexually; he is unfazed to discover that the 'woman' has a penis. A sex scene between Maria and Kynaston teases tenderly with male/female role play in both homosexual and heterosexual sex. The question of what is natural in gender attitudes and what is generic convention finds its political parallel in Charles II's simultaneously poignant and naïf comment to the theatrically deposed Kynaston: 'exile is a dreadful thing for one that knows his rightful place'. His comment misunderstands that monarchy is simply an agreement about role play and therefore every bit as determined by convention as is theatrical role play. There is no 'rightful place'.

Film adaptation and intertextuality

I add *Stage Beauty* to the discussion not just because of its *Othello*-centred plot and its contribution to a study of genre, but because of its cast. I have so far avoided giving the names of the actors in any of the films I have mentioned but we should now note the degree of overlap in terms of their roles and their role-history. Let us approach the films in approximately chronological order.

O was filmed in 1999 (see above for the delayed release). The director, Tim Blake Nelson, is experienced in adaptation from both sides of the camera: he was filming his role in the Coen brothers' adaptation of Homer, *O Brother, Where Art Thou?* at the same time he was editing *O* (according to the IMDb, the International Movie Data base). Julia Stiles, who played Desi, is experienced in Shakespeare adaptations, having starred as Kat Stratford in Gil Junger's update of *The Taming of the Shrew*, *Ten Things I Hate About You* (1999) and as Ophelia in Michael Almereyda's *Hamlet* (2000, sometimes called *Hamlet 2000*, starring Ethan Hawke as Hamlet). (For a comparative review of *O* and *Ten Things* see Alexander Leggatt, 'Teen Shakespeare'.) In 2001, Stiles played Sara in Thomas Carter's *Save the Last Dance* (released the same year as *O*) in which racial integration reverses the Othello scenario: when her mother dies, Sara moves to a ghetto area of Chicago to live with her father and finds herself one of the few white girls in a black school. Her happy interracial relationship with Derek contrasts with *O*'s tragic ending. Casting Stiles as Desi and then as Sara (or vice versa) offers viewers not just a dialogue between three Shakespeare films but a generic rewrite or remix of interracial dramas.

Josh Hartnett, who plays Hugo in *O* (2001) with his desire to fly and his envy of the hawk's pre-eminence, stars as a pilot, Captain Danny Walker, in Michael Bay's *Pearl Harbor* (also 2001) and as Sergeant Matthew Eversmann in Ridley Scott's *Black Hawk Down* (again 2001, my underlining), a film that centres on the courageous efforts to reach two downed US Black Hawk helicopters in Somalia. In both films, Hartnett plays heroic characters; his casting as Hugo offers a generic contrast. Hugo's desire to fly expresses a yearning for his previous/concurrent roles or, depending on the films' timings, looks forward to them.

Stage Beauty offers a similar nexus. As a period romance, it was regularly compared by reviewers to *Shakespeare in Love*. Its director, Richard Eyre, is a noted Shakespeare theatre director. Its female lead, Claire Danes, had starred as Juliet in Baz Luhrmann's *Romeo + Juliet* (1996). And Eamonn Walker, who plays John Othello in Andrew Davies' TV film, went on to play Othello in Shakespeare's play and language at the Globe in 2007.

There is a complex nexus here of associations, cross-references, allusions, precursors and successors. The difference between influence and coincidence can be hard to determine when films are released in the same year. But from an audience point of view it is hard not to read these actors' roles associatively – just as a Jacobean audience would have remembered Jonson's Thorello when watching Shakespeare's Othello and noted Burbage in both. My point here is that adaptations make a contribution to discussions of genre – not just the genre of adaptation but the genres and roles in which the actor has previously appeared. As a result, one cannot simply dismiss these films as 'Shakespeare lite'. Their complex and sophisticated harnessing of multiple allusions is perhaps best encapsulated in the title O where 'O' is not just an exclamation of surprise or dismay or revelation but the sound of joy Odin makes when he scores a point in basketball. As such it encapsulates in a single syllable the generic tensions we have been exploring throughout this chapter – between comedy and tragedy, between Elizabethan and modern. And in O, when Hugo and Odin are distracted and inattentive in a Shakespeare class, the English teacher singles them out with 'Would you care to name one of Shakespeare's poems for me'; Hugo's response is 'I thought he wrote movies'. Given the criss-crossing of material in this section, Hugo's response seems less flippant than it might. Shakespeare, it seems, did write movies.

Othello 1610

I want to end with brief mention of a production of *Othello* that drew attention not for Shakespeare's language but for a moment that lacked it. The production was not an adaptation but a production by Shakespeare's company of *Othello* in his own lifetime. In 1610 the King's Men performed two plays from their repertoire in Oxford: a brand-new city comedy by Ben Jonson, *The Alchemist*, and the relatively recent and obviously still popular tragedy, *Othello*. Henry Jackson, an Oxford fellow, described the King's Men's visit in a Latin letter to a friend:

> They also had tragedies, which they acted with propriety and fineness. In which [tragedies], not only through speaking but also through acting certain things, they moved [the audience] to tears. But truly the celebrated Desdemona, slain in our presence by her husband, although she pleaded her case very effectively throughout, yet moved [us] more after she was dead, when, lying on her bed, she entreated the pity of the spectators by her very countenance.
>
> (*Riverside Shakespeare*, 1852)

Jackson here distinguishes speech from action (as if speaking is not acting). Of all the things he could comment on in *Othello* – the colour of the Moor, the mixed marriage, the Machiavellian manipulations of Iago – it is interesting that what caught his attention was the emotional effect of the actor's body. The actor of Desdemona is complimented for his/her speech throughout but special praise is reserved for his/her ability to move us ('more') after her death by 'her very countenance'.

Paul Yachnin sees this spectator response as parallel to the play's 'shift from an aural to an ocular axis of relation', reminding us that the play moves from presenting a 'language-based relationship between the lovers at the outset to Othello's subsequent attempt to gain visual mastery over Desdemona' (Yachnin, 328). Tragedy, or at least the effect of tragedy, or at least the effect of *this* tragedy, does not reside purely in linguistic form – as we saw above in the film adaptations.

Writing matters

- Would *Othello* seem less comedic if Iago did not talk to the audience so much? Chart the progress of his soliloquies in terms of their effect on us (emotional, informational, comic). Now chart their frequency, noting the acts and scenes in which they appear: why do you think Iago talks to us less frequently as the play goes on? Is he losing control of the plot as events speed up? How does this accelerated momentum affect our relationship with him and his relationship with the play's genre(s)?

- Jealous husbands are the material of comedy as well as tragedy. (Shakespeare presents jealous husbands or suitors in *Merry Wives of Windsor*, *Much Ado about Nothing*, *Winter's Tale*, *Cymbeline*.) What would Shakespeare need to do (apart from changing the ending) to neutralize the tragic force of Othello's jealousy, making it a comic excess that gets corrected? Considering the modern films may help here: what do they have in common with the play? Do they have the same or different moments when the plot might have taken a different turn? Do they have language that comes back to haunt a character or gets recycled by another?

- Desdemona accepts responsibility for her tragic end; Iago says nothing. Why do you think the master wordsmith Iago suddenly falls silent? Why do you think Desdemona says 'Nobody. I myself' in response to Emilia's question 'who hath done / This deed?' (5.2.121–2). How does this linguistically submissive act fit with the linguistically feisty Desdemona we have met earlier?

CHAPTER THREE

Language and boundaries

Othello is a play that is unusually conscious of differences, doubleness, binaries, borders, overlaps, duplications and separations at all levels: plot, metaphor, vocabulary. Its central couple is different in age and in colour. Iago's manipulation turns an innocent wife into a perceived adulteress. Brabantio insists that we are in a civilized city, not wild countryside ('This is Venice: / My house is not a grange' (1.1.104–5)). The play has two locations, the political city-state of Venice and an island associated with love, Aphrodite's Cyprus. It offers contradictory narratives: of the Turkish naval fleet, of the handkerchief. It has two time schemes. It has a villain who swears by Janus, the god of doors and thresholds, a god who looks backwards and forwards simultaneously. It endows formal action (such as Cassio's kissing of his fingers) with fantastic meanings (Serpieri, 137). The political plot is about Turks versus Venetians. The 'Turk' was a byword for the 'infidel' and the Turks are conveniently drowned by the start of Act Two, closing the martial plot. But Act Two opens with Iago's satiric quayside misogyny about women, concluding with the comic protest that it 'is true, or else I am a Turk' (2.1.114). We know that his statements are not true; the natural corollary is that Iago is a Turk. Turks and Venetians are thus not entirely separate categories. Separation and conflation of categories is something we have seen again and again in the play.

The linguistic locus of this multiplicity, contradiction, duality and liminality is, obviously, Iago. In Chapters One and Two we looked at how these items worked in the two different spheres of Narrative and Genre. In this chapter I want to locate them in the larger category of boundaries, with a particular focus on Iago's language. Iago is able to manipulate meaning because he is manipulatively aware of the polysemous quality of language. He is not just a double-dealer, but one who linguistically deals in doubles: the pun, paradox, repetition, echoes.

Iago and thresholds

A. D. Nuttall wrote that Othello is the tragedy of 'a hero who went into a house' (Nuttall, 279). Tony Tanner said something similar: Othello is 'all at sea in a house' (Tanner 2010, 530). That is indeed part of the problem: Othello is a military man, has lived his life in camps until 'nine moons wasted' (1.3.85), is an 'extravagant and wheeling stranger' (*extravagant*: travelling outside the usual confines, from the Latin *vagare*, to travel; 1.1.134). In Venice he travels into new territory: domesticity, marriage, the house.

But that is not the real problem. The problem is, as Patricia Dorval observes, that Othello makes Iago his doorkeeper. Iago swears by Janus – the Roman god of gates and doorways, whose symbol is a double-faced head, facing in opposite directions. (For an analysis of Iago's association with Janus see Dorval's careful review of 'threshold aesthetics' in Oliver Parker's 1995 film of *Othello*.)

Iago's space is the liminal. He is and is not in love with Desdemona:

Now I do love her [Desdemona] too;
Not out of absolute lust ...

(2.1.292)

and he is and is not cuckolded by Othello:

> it is thought abroad that 'twixt my sheets
> H'as done my office. I know not if it be true ...

$$(1.3.378-9)$$

Throughout the play he faces in two directions: he appears honest, acts deceitfully. He controls the play's thresholds – of genre, language, and meaning. He patrols the play's linguistic boundaries and he controls interpretation. When Othello demands 'proof' of Desdemona's infidelity (3.3.194), Iago promises to lead Othello to the 'door of truth' (3.3.410). Tanner rightly queries the phrase: why only *to* the door? (Tanner 2010, 521). One answer is that Iago is the doorkeeper, the one who polices the boundary between truth and non-truth.

We might compare him here with other doorkeepers in Shakespeare: clowns. In *Comedy of Errors*, Dromio of Ephesus is the doorkeeper. He is the clown-servant of Antipholus of Ephesus and part of the play's farce arises when his twin brother, Dromio of Syracuse, shows up unbeknown to him, is claimed by the Ephesian Dromio's fiancée, and installed as doorkeeper in his place. 'Go, get thee from the door' is the Syracusan servant's command to the knocking at the door, and the rightful Ephesian servant protests in bewilderment: 'What patch is made our porter? ... O villain, thou hast stol'n both mine office and my name' (3.1.36, 44). In *Taming of the Shrew* one of the first jobs of Petruccio's clowning servant, Grumio, is to knock at the entrance to Hortensio's house: 'knock me at this gate / And rap me well, or I'll knock your knave's pate' (1.2.12–13). The clown, Peter the servant, in *Romeo and Juliet* has liberty (or gives himself liberty) to extend invitations to the Capulets' party but he knows where to draw the line: 'If you be not of the house of Montagues I pray come and crush a cup of wine' (1.2.81–2). The porter in *Macbeth* keeps the gate of Macbeth's castle and, he implies, of a medieval hellmouth (2.3.17). The scene opens with frantic knocking, and the porter takes 20 lines to tell us about his function as gatekeeper before opening the gate.

Since clowns guard boundaries, it is appropriate that they function as the play's go-betweens. The clownish servant, Speed, takes love messages from Valentine to Silvia in *Two Gentlemen of Verona*; Costard carries letters from Berowne and from Armado to Rosaline and Jaquenetta in *Love's Labour's Lost*; Feste, the fool, travels between Olivia's and Orsino's courts in *Twelfth Night*; the comic servant, Lancelot Gobbo, moves from Shylock's household to Bassanio's in *Merchant of Venice*. Clowns do not just guard one boundary; they themselves move and transact between two houses or characters.

Othello has a clown who appears only briefly, in 3.1 and 3.4. In the first of these scenes, the Clown is the household porter who pays Cassio's musicians to go away: 'the general so likes your music that he desires you, for love's sake, to make no more noise with it. ... If you have any music that may not be heard, to't again' (3.1.11–6). In the second scene, the Clown is asked to act as a go-between between Desdemona and Cassio ('Seek him out, bid him come hither, tell him I have moved my lord on his behalf'; 3.4.18–19).

At only 20 lines each, both scenes are short but they are linguistically important. The first scene exists only for its pun on 'honest'; the second exists only for its pun on 'lies'. In the first we have the following dialogue:

Cassio.	Dost thou hear, mine honest friend?
Clown.	No, I hear not your honest friend, I hear you.
Cassio.	Prithee keep up thy quillets [quibbles].

(3.1.21–2)

And in the second:

Desdemona.	Do you know, sirrah, where lieutenant Cassio lies?
Clown.	I dare not say he lies anywhere.

(3.4.1–2)

Both the adjective 'honest' and the verb 'lies' will be appropriated by the play's unofficial clown, the linguistic Janus who controls the play's 'quillets'. Iago manipulates appearances so that others associate him with the word 'honest': characters call him 'honest Iago' at 1.3.295, 2.3.173, 2.3.330 and 5.2.72, as if that were his full name, and his 'honesty' is regularly referred to. And he plays with the verb 'lie' in a more calculating way than the play's Clown:

Othello.	What hath he said?
Iago.	Faith, that he did – I know not what. He did –
Othello.	What? What?
Iago.	Lie.
Othello.	With her?
Iago.	With her, on her, what you will.

(4.1.31–3)

Punning on the verb 'lie' is what clowns do. Hamlet has the following conversation with his play's clown, the gravedigger:

Hamlet.	Whose grave's this, sirrah?
Gravedigger.	Mine, sir ...
Hamlet.	I think it be thine indeed, for thou liest in't.
Gravedigger.	You lie out on't, sir, and therefore 'tis not yours. For my part, I do not lie in't, yet it is mine.
Hamlet.	Thou dost lie in't, to be in't and say 'tis thine. 'Tis for the dead, not for the quick: therefore thou liest.
Gravedigger.	'Tis a quick lie, sir, 'twill away again from me to you.

(5.1.115–25)

Hamlet is often described as the Clown in *Hamlet*, the character aware of language's doubleness, the character who speaks in puns until he meets his match in the play's official Clown, the gravedigger, whereupon he realizes 'we must speak by the card or equivocation will undo us'; 5.1.133–4). The pun links Hamlet with the Clown. It also links Iago with the Clown.

The problem with the Clown in *Othello*, as everyone notices, is that he is so unfunny. Emrys Jones says that he is 'miserably lacking in entertainment value' (Jones 1971, 139). Peter Holland remarks, 'No one has much good to say about Othello's Clown: critics usually ignore him completely, productions usually cut him' (Holland, 126). (The scenes' *raison d'être*, Holland argues, is only to provide a role for the actor Robert Armin, the specialist clown in Shakespeare's company; Holland, 127–8.) Trevor Nunn's 1989 RSC production was one of the most successful of modern treatments, placing the Clown smoothly in the production's Edwardian setting. Nunn cast the Clown as one of a small group of military subalterns, guarding Othello's and Desdemona's quarters. When requested by the subaltern to leave, Cassio changes his tactic from providing music for Desdemona to requesting speech with Emilia: he asks the subaltern to summon Emilia. The subaltern accepts the request with clear condescension as the group looks at Cassio, speculating pruriently about his request. Focusing on class, and dispensing with clowning in any conventional sense, the subaltern's witticisms were passive-aggressive jibes at a cashiered superior.

Productions that cut the Clown ignore the way his role paves the way for Iago's, both linguistically and dramaturgically. The mid-line stage direction below shows us the sequence in 3.1 in which Cassio bids goodbye to one clown as he welcomes another:

> *Cassio.*   Do good my friend. (*Exit Clown.*) In happy time, Iago.
>
> (3.1.30)

The Clown exits just as Iago arrives: the latter replaces the former, using his tactics, occupying his place. Iago may not be promoted to military lieutenant in the plot, but he is a lieutenant (*lieu-tenant*: literally, place-holder) in the play's comic dramaturgy.

Iago and hendiadys

Let us turn to some of the linguistic quillets whose doubleness Iago exploits. I begin with the rhetorical figure, hendiadys (the noun comes from a Greek phrase meaning 'one through two'). Rather than using an adjective and a noun to describe a single concept, hendiadys uses two nouns joined by 'and': 'sound and fury' for instance, in *Macbeth* 5.5.27, or 'tediousness and process' in *Richard II* 2.3.11–12. Hendiadys can also couple two adjectives (Othello's 'free and bounteous', 'serious and great', 'speculative and officed' in 1.3.266–71) or two verbs ('corrupt and taint' in the same speech). However, nouns comprise the most common pairings: Othello fetches his 'life and being' from royal men (1.2.21), is unwilling to exchange bachelor freedom for 'circumscription and confine' (1.2.27), speaks of 'place and exhibition' (1.3.238), of 'accommodation and besort' (1.3.239), of 'wordly matter and direction' (1.3.300). These examples come from George T. Wright's study of hendiadys in Shakespeare; he counts 28 examples in *Othello*, the highest Shakespeare total after *Hamlet* (Wright, 173). Hendiadys is common in the work of Virgil, the Roman poet (70–19 BCE) from whom Shakespeare presumably learned and adopted this rhetorical figure.

It is important to note the small word that is central in hendiadys: *and*. This, Wright says, is an important word in life for helping us get our bearings; we rely on *and*, it reassures us, it is 'a word we take as signaling a coordinate structure, a parallelism of thought and meaning' (Wright, 169). We expect 'small grammatical units joined by *and* to be parallel not only in grammar but also in bearing. *They ought, we feel, to face in the same direction*' (Wright, 170, my italics). Wright's image here accords with our discussion about Janus in the previous section of this chapter. In *Othello*, Iago's words and linguistic structures do not face in the same direction because, as a character ruled by Janus, neither does he.

We see this in his use of 'and', independently of the conjunction's use in hendiadys. Early in the play, he lays his cards on the table about motive:

> I hate the Moor
> And it is thought abroad that 'twixt my sheets
> He's done my office.

> (1.3.385–7)

As almost all critics have noted, it is easy to mistake the conjunctive for the causal here, to assume that 'and' means 'because'. Maybe Iago means us to do so. Hatred of the Moor because of rumours ('it is thought abroad') that he has cuckolded Iago ("twixt my sheet he's done / My office') is logical (if not laudable). There is a cause and effect from past wrong to current attitude. But Iago joins the two together in a reverse fashion: the effect (hatred) precedes the cause (illicit sex) which calls into question the causality of the emotion, hatred. With such a misleading use of 'and', it behoves us to pay attention to how the play uses hendiadys.

Iago is not the only character to use hendiadys in *Othello* but he uses it differently. In fact, it is often difficult to know whether his use of 'and' actually joins two related things or merely tricks us into thinking they are related. Here is a list from the first scene:

Iago
pride and purposes (11)
be-leed and calmed (29)
letter and affection (35)
duteous and knee-crooking (44)
forms and visage (49)
act and figure (61)

night and negligence (75)
flag and sign (154)

The variety of use and meaning in Iago's hendiadys can be seen by looking at how Roderigo and Brabantio use hendiadys in the same scene.

Roderigo
simple and pure (106)
odd-even and dull (121)
bold and saucy (126)
extravagant and wheeling (134)

Brabantio
full of supper and distempering draughts (98)
My spirit and my place (102)

The yokings of hendiadys are often a side-effect of the English language, whose unusual capacity for synonymous phrasing is a result of English having imported terms from Latin and French for use alongside the native Anglo Saxon. The second term is sometimes repetitive or redundant because synonymous. This is the case with Roderigo's *simple and pure* and his *bold and saucy*. At other times the two terms are complementary: Brabantio's *supper and distempering draughts* = food and drink; *my spirit and my place* = character and social position; Roderigo's *odd-even and dull* = on the border of night and day when things are lifeless.

   The two terms in Iago's uses of hendiadys are more complex. Some of them are certainly synonyms. But they are generally used in a greater variety of ways. And across the play the two terms sometimes do not fit together; sometimes they even pull in opposite directions. The reassuring conjunction 'and' misleads us into taking its function as genuinely conjunctive. Wright's comment about Shakespeare – that his 'examples [of hendiadys] are dazzlingly various' (Wright, 169) is actually more true of Iago.

In the last example from Iago in scene 1, above, Iago follows his hendiadys with a pun:

> I must show out a flag and sign of love,
> Which is indeed but sign.

(1.1.154–5)

(A paraphrase: I must display a flag and military banner ('sign') of love which is in fact only an appearance ('but sign')).

The pun is the opposite of hendiadys: if hendiadys collapses two into one, the pun expands one into two. In two consecutive lines, Iago uses two oppositional rhetorical figures.

In *Hamlet*, hendiadys and puns are not just opposite rhetorical figures but opposed strategies. Claudius is the arch-conflater, speaking in figures that yoke incompatibles – oxymoron, paradox, hendiadys; Hamlet is the provocative comedian who uses puns to deconstruct his stepfather's meaning. *Hamlet* is a play about unusual yokings. Claudius' marriage to his sister-in-law makes him a father-uncle, Gertrude a mother-aunt. His military plans keep the ammunitions factory working 24 hours a day, yoking together not only day and night (making 'the night joint-labourer with the day'; 1.1.81) but also weekdays and restdays: '[he] does not divide the Sunday from the week' (1.1.79). It is appropriate that his characteristic rhetorical figures are those which put two things together.

Hamlet's tactic is to question the new and unnatural couplings through the rhetorical figure I have defined as the opposite of hendiadys: the pun. In Act One his puns on son/sun and kin/kind strenuously resist the new semantic and emotional relationships.

This is clear and straightforward: Hamlet is Claudius' enemy; their lexicons are also at odds. But how can Iago use hendiadys in one line and a pun in the next? How can he oppose himself? To answer this question we need to move from hendiadys to the pun.

Iago and puns

In this section I want to think about the pun as the linguistic form that characterizes Iago. The *OED* defines *pun* as 'the use of a word in such a way as to suggest two or more meanings or different associations, or of two or more words of the same or nearly the same sound with different meanings, so as to produce a humorous effect; a play on words' (*n.* 1). The word *pun* first occurs in the English language in 1644 (its etymology is unknown). Any earlier reference to puns used the classical rhetorical forms: *paronomasia* or *prosonomasia* in Greek and, in Latin, *adnominatio* or *agnominatio* (see the anonymous *Ad Herennium* 4.21–2, 29–31; Abraham Fraunce 1588). Classical *paronomasia* is slightly more capacious than the English pun. Whereas the latter is one word with two meanings, paronomasia also includes two words with similar sounds: this form 'emphasizes a resemblance but not identity of sounds, as in the "O fate, O fault" of Sidney's sonnet 93. The effect is partly musical in somewhat the way that assonance is' (Dundas, 223).

The pun is a rhetorical figure although, as Simon Palfrey notes, it is an unusual one. All rhetorical figures have an aim: to persuade intellectually or to create emotion in the hearer. The pun has only a local effect: 'it is understood as a frivolous sideshow' (Palfrey, 135). Consequently, classical writers advocated that it be used frugally. Another incongruity of the pun is that it relies on ambiguity; rhetoric usually requires disambiguation. (Some classical thinkers felt that ambiguity was a deficiency in language and therefore disapproved of the pun.) Since the creation of ambiguity is Iago's linguistic tour de force, this is a highly appropriate rhetorical tool for him to use.

In pursuing this topic we need first to disburden ourselves of the modern understanding of puns as funny (or, in our more recent view, unfunny.) They *can* be comic in Elizabethan drama, especially within the genre of comedy.

But if we look at classical and Renaissance rhetoricians' understanding of wordplay, we can begin to grasp the pun's non-comic sphere.

The Roman orator Cicero (106 BCE to 43 BCE) stressed the polarity of the two words being played upon; the key point was that 'similar words express dissimilar things' (Dundas, 223). The rhetorician Quintilian (c. 35 CE to c. 100 CE) noted the concept of dialogue in puns' construction of meaning, 'one word being of the speaker's own selection while the other is supplied by his opponent' (Dundas, 224). Punning offers a competition for meaning, a struggle between two claimants as to whose interpretative system will prevail. (This may lie behind Palfrey's observation that wit in punning is located in the hearer rather than the speaker since it is the hearer who holds, and adjudicates, two meanings.)

Following the classical *paronomasia*, the Renaissance understood as puns those verbal tricks that we would identify by other names or descriptions. In *Romeo and Juliet*, the punning of the character Mercutio is based on 'internal declensions': *dream/drum*; *knees/nose*; *team/atom* (Garnier-Giamarchi, 141). We would recognize other Renaissance puns as the rhetorical trick in which the same word is used as a different part of speech or with a different meaning – as when Iago describes Roderigo as 'this poor trash of Venice, whom I trash for his quick hunting' (2.1.301–2). Still others we would recognize simply as syntactical balancing or Euphuism (an elaborate prose style, very popular in the late sixteenth century, characterized by alliteration, parallelism, and antitheses; the name comes from the character Euphues in John Lyly's *Euphues, the Anatomy of his Wit* (1578)). Judith Dundas gives the following examples from Sir Philip Sidney's *Arcadia*:

What can *saying* make them believe whom *seeing* cannot persuade?

(Sidney, *Arcadia*, 92)

thou hast employed my love there where all love is
deserved, and for recompense has sent me more love than
ever I *desired*.

(Sidney, Arcadia, 85)

It is a short step from here to Hamlet's 'A little more than kin,
and less than kind' (1.2.65).

Simon Palfrey distinguishes between puns in comedy
(localized quibbling, creating an affinity between audience and
speaker) and puns in tragedy where characters are unaware of
the puns they speak and puns are not about 'dizzying display'
but about 'the spoken moment bearing multiple lines of
possible unfurling' (Palfrey, 112). What Palfrey calls the 'basic
architecture of a pun' is essentially tragic:

> It is multiple, folded, or at cross-purposes; things lurk
> or move at angles; it beckons toward different pasts and
> possibilities; it evokes alternatives within predetermination.
> (Palfrey, 111)

Unlike the pun in comedy, where the effect is courted by the
speaker and creates a relationship with the hearers (including
us), the tragic pun is uttered to no one, functioning independently within a speech and within the play like echo and
allusion (Palfrey, 129).

Jonathan Culler says something similar to Palfrey: a pun
makes language respond to 'the call of the phoneme, whose
echoes tell of wild realms beyond the code' (a phoneme is the
smallest sound unit in a language 'that can distinguish one
word from another (e.g. /p/ and /b/ in English *pat, bat*)'; *OED*,
'phoneme' 1b. See Culler, introduction to *On Puns*, quoted by
Garnier-Gimachi, 144). Using Gregory Ulmer's coinage, the
'puncept', Philippa Berry explains how 'the pun can function
as a 'puncept' in its formation of new concepts which may
hint at another order of knowledge' (Berry, 59). *Hinting* at
another order of *knowledge* – this is Iago in a nutshell.

It is interesting to see how many critics describe the pun in non-linguistic, metaphoric ways. For Michael Neill, it is a verbal bed-trick: about substitution, the wrong person (Neill 1984, 124). It is therefore a particularly apt figure for *Othello* which activates a bed-trick not physically (as in *Measure for Measure* and *All's Well that Ends Well*) but linguistically, via Iago's (repeated) aural illusions. Tony Tanner offers a variant of Neill's image when he likens a pun to 'an adulterous bed in which two meanings that should be separated are coupled together' (1979, 53). When Emma Smith writes (of Cassio's function as go-between in the courtship of Desdemona and Othello) that 'there were always three people in this marriage' (Smith 2005, 10), one is reminded not just of Princess Diana's 1995 television interview whose phrasing Smith cleverly appropriates, but of Geoffrey Hartman's analysis of puns:

> You can define a pun as two meanings competing for the same phonemic space or as one sound bringing forth semantic twins, but, however you look at it, *it's a crowded situation.*
>
> (Hartman, 347, my italics)

Two in a bed; the wrong two in a bed. Two in a word; the wrong two in a word. No wonder that Iago, the architect of the false wife story, uses as his agent misleading words.

Iago as pun

In *The Garden of Eloquence* (1577), the Renaissance rhetorician Henry Peacham called the pun a 'light and illuding form' (Peacham, 56). The OED glosses 'illuding' as 'mocking'. The word comes from *ludere*, to play; this Latin verb gives us our words 'ludic' (playful), 'illusion' (deception, false appearance, the act of being mocked), 'allusion' (originally this meant a game; now it means a passing reference), 'delusion' (the act of cheating or mocking). We no longer use the word 'illuding' – 'illusive' and 'illusionary' are probably our closest modern equivalents. Perhaps because he views the pun as 'light and illuding', Peacham advocates that it not be overused, especially 'in grave and weightie causes' (Peacham, 56, Dundas, 225). The scholar Julius Caesar Scaliger (1484–1588) said much the same: it is not suitable for serious poetry. But it is, he says, appropriate for epigrams, satires, comedies (Dundas 225). *Othello* is both a 'grave and weightie' tragedy and a comedy. And its comic villain uses illuding language to effect tragic destruction.

But it is too reductive simply to say that *Othello* is a play in which Iago's principal agent of destruction is the pun. In one sense, Iago is the human embodiment of the pun – a sign (ensign) who 'hints at another order of knowledge' as Berry said above of the pun, a character who works by echo and allusion, as Palfrey said above of the pun, a Janus-figure who looks in two directions. 'I am not what I am' (1.1.64) is a definition of the pun. Like the pun, Iago fractures correspondence. Like the pun, he is impossible to pin down, whether linguistically or psychologically. 'Men should be what they seem', Iago tells Othello (3.3.129). Like the pun, Iago is not what he seems.

Puns versus metaphors

If Iago is the pun, Othello is metaphor. It is not unusual to characterize these two characters in rhetorical terms: critics have identified Othello as hyperbole (the rhetorical figure of exaggeration) and Iago as litotes (the rhetorical figure of understatement). Act One tells us that Othello is 'an extravagant and wheeling stranger / Of here and everywhere' (1.1.134–5). Extravagance is the keynote definition of metaphor. As I mentioned above, extravagance literally means travelling outside one's normal bounds; similarly, metaphor means being carried across.

Othello's identity is founded on metaphor. Palfrey notes: 'every role and name he has worn has, in some sense, been borrowed' (Palfrey, 35). Palfrey makes this observation after analysing Othello's final speech, his 'self-epitaph', in which he locates himself in a series of correspondences with Others: a base Indian (or, in the Folio reading, Judean), an Arabian tree, a malignant Turk, a Venetian, and a circumcised dog. This not only confirms what we suspected all along, that there 'is' no stable Othello identity, but illustrates Othello's 'sequential displacing and discovery of self into others [as] a self-constitution (and dissolution) through metaphor'. Palfrey links this unstable identity to the working of metaphor itself – metaphor stands for 'some primary cohering reality: but the only access to and presence of this reality is the metaphors' (Palfrey, 35).

These sequential attempts at correspondence indicate the ontological difficulty Othello has had throughout the play, as race critics have noted in other terms. Andrew Hadfield sees Othello's conflicted identity as an example of the play's 'fear that the boundaries between self and other are not as rigid as they might be' (Hadfield, 229). Othello tries to be absorbed by his new society but is always Other; in Homi Bhaba's terms, he is 'almost the same but not quite' (Bhaba, 86). This is as apt a description of metaphor as it is of Othello.

Iago, the punster, locates his self in separation ('I am not what I am'; 1.1.65) whereas in his last speech, with its multiple attempts to define the 'I', Othello is still attempting metaphorically to create connection.

The Iago music

When we talk about language in *Othello* we think of the (now almost clichéd) 'Othello music' identified by G. Wilson

Knight. Othello speaks like the exotic epic hero he is. He uses grandiloquent images: the Pontic sea at 3.3.45, the cosmic eclipse at 5.2.98. He laments in rhythmic roars: 'O insupportable, O heavy hour!' (5.2.107). He uses calmly balanced syntax and similes: 'It gives me wonder great as my content / To see you here before me!' (2.1.181–2). He extinguishes a fight simply through language: 'Keep up your bright swords, for the dew will rust them' (1.2.59). He uses extravagant vocabulary: 'exsufflicate' at 3.3.185 is one of many words in the play which are unique in Shakespeare and which receive their first English use in the Shakespeare canon. (What does 'exsufflicate' mean? It comes from the Latin infinitive, *exsufflare* = to blow up; attached here as an adjective to 'surmises', it presumably means, as Honigmann glosses it, albeit with a query, '(?) inflated, i.e. improbable'; 3.3.185n).

If we think back to classical rhetoric, we recall Judith Dundas' summary of paronomasia, quoted at the start of this chapter: '*the effect is partly musical* in somewhat the way that assonance is' (Dundas, 223, my italics). Given that Iago functions paronomastically we may perhaps speak of the Iago music.

'Slipper and subtle' language

With puns, language multiplies, loses ties with its referent(s). In *Othello* this expands beyond the pun to language generally.

After the brawl in Act Two, Iago's language clears Cassio of involvement while simultaneously pointing the finger at him:

I had rather have this tongue cut from my mouth
Than it should do offence to Michael Cassio,
Yet I persuade myself to speak the truth
Shall nothing wrong him.

(2.3.217–20)

Truth in Iago's language is misapplied or misdescribed, just as the reverse happens, with lies masquerading as the truth. He creates circumstances in which truth is not seen for what it is.

Iago has no need to alter meaning by lying. Repetition is enough ('By heaven, thou echo'st me', exclaims Othello in exasperation at 3.3.109). So too is prepositional substitution ('with her, on her'; 4.1.34). So too is negative avowal: 'I speak not yet of proof'. So too is hypothesis ('What if I had said I had seen him do you wrong?'; 4.1.24). And note here the improbability of this conjecture: Iago's construction implies that he has seen Cassio and Desdemona have sex, something he later tells Othello is impossible when he asks the general if he would grossly gape while Cassio tops Desdemona (3.3.397–8).

From here Iago's linguistic tactics affect the entire play which becomes a tissue of repetition and echoes and contradiction. Iago says Cassio is a 'slipper and subtle knave' (2.1.239–40); that Desdemona is a 'super-subtle Venetian' (1.3.357).

Our auditory bafflement and confusion works at the smallest units. The Duke promises Brabantio 'the bloody book of law' (1.3.68). Tony Tanner questions the adjective: 'bloody' is the opposite of law; the law is designed to prevent bloodshed (Tanner 2010, 517). In soliloquy Iago confides that he will make Othello grateful for 'practising upon his peace and quiet / Even to madness' (2.1.301–2). The (grammatical) question is: whose madness? What are we to make of the Egyptian who 'could almost read / The thoughts of people' (3.4.58–60). The qualifying adverb is odd: either one can read the thoughts of people or one cannot – it is not a partial talent.

Othello tells of his 'demerits' (1.2.22). The word means both 'merits' (which is how Othello seems to use it here) and its opposite: deficiencies. As so often in language, it is context that determines meaning. Iago exploits this ambiguity of language and elevates it to a tactic, turning merits into demerits, things into their opposites. The result is to evacuate all words of semantic content – even colourless words, as we shall see, like the verb 'to be' – and reduce the play, like its hero, to an interpretative impasse:

> I think my wife be honest, and think she is not.
> I think that thou art just, and think thou art not.

> (3.3.387–8)

The verb 'think' is important here. Language specialists consider this verb as encoding 'median probability' (Eggins and Slade, 102): the judgement being expressed is distanced from the speaker. Othello is saying he thinks something but does not know what to think.

Hearing

The hero, like the audience, is vulnerable because the ear is not an orifice over which we have any control. This is why sound effects in theatre are more dangerous than visual effects: spectators can avert their eyes; they cannot avert their ears. A famous Stratford production of *Titus Andronicus* in 1955 had a high incidence of audience fainting, not because of the play's blood and gore, which was represented in a stylized fashion with red ribbons, but because of a memorable sound effect: Titus' amputation of his hand was accompanied by the offstage sound of chicken bones being crunched.

In the Senate scene the Duke offers Brabantio paradoxical *sententiae* (proverbial wisdom) by way of consolation:

> When remedies are past the griefs are ended
> By seeing the worst which late on hopes depended.

> (1.3.203–4)

Brabantio dismisses them, saying that the *sententiae* are 'equivocal' to 'sugar or to gall', that is, inducing equally peace or bile (1.3.217–18). Brabantio concludes 'But words are words: I never yet did hear / That the bruised heart was pierced through the ear' (1.3.219–20).

The first aphorism is a truncated form of an Elizabethan proverb – 'words are but words' – implying consolingly that they are merely words, hence harmless. The play will show (Iago will show) that there is nothing harmless about words, just as it will show that hearts can be pierced via the ear. Brabantio here is using 'pierced' in the sense of 'cured'. Honigmann glosses the line 'I never yet did hear / That the bruised heart was pierced through the ear' as '[I never heard] that the crushed heart was relieved by mere words that reach it through the ear' (1.3.220n). The sense is that the heart is reached via the ear and therefore comforted by the phrases it hears. But piercing the heart can also mean the opposite in Shakespeare – the meaning we would associate logically with the verb 'pierce', where it causes hurt not healing. In *Midsummer Night's Dream* the rejected Demetrius tells Hermia that he is 'pierced through the heart with [her] stern cruelty' (3.2.59). Thomas Mowbray makes the same complaint in *Richard II*: he is 'pierced to the soul with slander's venom'd spear, / The which no balm can cure but his [Henry Bolingbroke's] heart-blood / Which breathed this poison' (*Richard II* 1.1.171–3). In *Titus Andronicus* we hear that Titus's bereavement 'hath pierced him deep and scarred his heart' (*Titus Andronicus* 4.4.31). But in *Othello* words are, like the hero, of a 'free and open nature' (1.3.398), enjoying an 'unhoused free condition' (1.2.26).

The human instinct is to disambiguate. We use context to calculate probabilities as to whether 'demerits' means its opposite or whether the situation requires us to activate piercing's healing rather than hurtful meaning. Throughout the play Iago thwarts this basic cognitive ability in Othello – he opens up meanings. Or rather: he controls disambiguation so that Othello activates the wrong meaning.

George Puttenham, the Elizabethan author of *The Art of English Poesie* (1589), said that the greatest victory is when one triumphs over another person's mind. This is Iago's triumph and it is shown in Othello's transfer of trust from his wife to his ensign. The kneeling episode at the end of 3.3 in which Othello and Iago dedicate themselves to revenge is a quasi-marriage, concluding with a nuptial exchange: 'Now art thou my lieutenant' / 'I am your own for ever' (3.3.481–2). But Iago's triumph over Othello's mind is also shown in Othello's linguistic change. As we saw in Chapter 2, Othello has much in common linguistically with Tamburlaine, that epic Marlovian hero who conquers simply by countermanding; the Persian lord who switches to Tamburlaine's side explains that he is 'Won with thy words and conquered with thy looks' (*1 Tamburlaine* 1.2.228), a line that could also be uttered by Desdemona. Iago's triumph over his general is to conquer Othello's controlled syntax and similes. He reduces him to the asyndetic (*asyndeton* is the rhetorical term for the omission of conjunctions): 'Handkerchief! Confessions! Handkerchief!' (4.1.37), to the illogical ('first to be hanged, and then to confess'; 4.1.38–9), to the theriologic (*theriologic* means 'pertaining to beasts'): 'goats and monkeys' (4.1.263) and to the inarticulate (he foams at the mouth in 4.1.54). If, as Ben Jonson said (echoing the ancients), 'language most shows a man' (Hereford and Simpsons, 8:625) Othello's being is assaulted (and the assault is visible/audible) in language.

In the next few sections I want to look at Iago's manipulation of small words.

To be (or not to be)

As we saw in Chapter 1, Iago's language is notable for its careful use and insidious colonization of small words. One of the small words that Iago manipulates is the verb 'to be'. 'I am not what I am', he confides to Roderigo (1.1.64). Negating not only meaning but being, he is, as critics point out, the opposite of God, who says 'I am that I am' (Exodus 3.14). He is also the opposite of Hamlet. Hamlet defends his grief as more than seeming: 'Nay, madam, it *is*; I know not seems' (1.2.76, my italics). Iago knows not 'is'. Thus, correspondence is fractured, identity attacked, and linguistic, narrative and interpretative confidence collapses. We move from the cryptic 'I am not what I am' to the riddling 'Were I the Moor, I would not be Iago' (1.1.56). By Act Four Iago runs rings round this verb. Speaking about Othello's personality and behaviour, he says: 'He's that he *is*: I may not breathe my censure / What he might *be*; if what he might [*sc. be*], he *is* not, / I would to heaven he *were!*' (4.1.270–2). The language is dizzying here with its changes of tense. (Antony Sher, who played Iago for the Royal Shakespeare Company in 2004, describes how in performance he emphasized these 'cryptic comments' with 'a little singsong rhythm'; Sher, 67.) In an earlier tragedy, *Romeo and Juliet*, such cryptic comments would have earned a crisp dismissal: 'Riddling confession finds but riddling shrift' (2.3.52). In *Othello* such riddles are the play's currency.

Iago's statement to Roderigo that 'Were I the Moor, I would not be Iago' is followed by an explanation: 'In following him I follow but myself' (1.1.56–7). Honigmann glosses these lines with clarity: 'Were I the Moor, I would not wish to be Iago. [But, being Iago,] I only follow him to follow my own interests' (1.1.56–7n). Iago's explanation at this point repeats his opening statement in this speech: 'I follow him to serve my turn upon him' (1.1.41). But although Iago twice explains that he follows Othello to serve his 'turn', he does not yet tell Roderigo (or us) what that turn might be. Indeed, given his opportunistic and improvisatory actions, it is probable that he himself does not yet know; in later soliloquies we see him working things out ('How? Let's see'; 1.3.393; ''Tis here, but yet confused'; 2.1.309). When, in later dialogue with Othello, we see what the 'turn' is (the death of Desdemona), Iago never explains why.

'To be' denotes transparency; that is what '*is*' means, the divine linguistic and ontological correspondence of God's 'I am that I am'. As we saw in Chapter 1, the fall was linguistic:

in Eden, word and thing were in perfect harmony. Once 'to be' is fractured, meaning collapses. In just a few scenes, Othello moves from the interpretative confidence of 'My life upon her faith' (1.3.295) and 'if she be false, O then heaven mocks itself!' (3.3.282) to the interpretative paralysis of 'I think my wife be honest, and think she is not, / I think that thou art just, and think thou art not' (3.3.287–8). He no longer knows what to think or believe because Iago has driven a wedge between words and meaning. That wedge starts in scene 1 when he destabilizes the verb 'to be'.

Verdi's Iago sings his 'Credo in un Dio crudel' (I believe in a cruel God). He states, 'I am a man and therefore wicked'. (Emotions and motivation are much simpler in the world of opera!) Verdi's Iago here uses language to assert what 'I am'; that is precisely the correspondence that ceases to function in Shakespeare's play.

We might also note that 'to be' is the slipperiest verb in the English language because it changes its shape grammatically; it is no coincidence that it is a tool of Iago, the play's slipperiest character.

Modal verbs

I said above that Iago's control is over small words such as verbs. A category of verb that is underexamined is the modal auxiliary. In manipulating it, Iago reigns supreme.

In English, modal verbs (also called modal auxiliaries because they are used with other verbs) are: *can*; *could*; *may*; *might*; *shall*; *should*; *will*; *would*; *must* (*mote* is obsolete). *Ought* is not identical in form because it requires an infinitive but it is identical in the modality it expresses (compulsion) and so it is often included in lists of modals, sometimes with the qualifier 'semi-modal'.

In Act 3, scene 1 of *Coriolanus* (1607) the imperious Coriolanus crosses words with one of the tribunes of the people, Sicinius. Sicinius is trying to curb Coriolanus's poisonous (as he sees it) influence over the common people:

> It is a mind
> That shall remain a poison where it is,
> Not poison any further.

(3.1.86–8)

Coriolanus, who is elsewhere easily influenced by small words in this play, reacts to the verb 'shall':

Coriolanus.   Shall remain?
                Hear you this Triton of the minnows?
    [minor sea god of minor fish] Mark you
                His absolute 'shall'?
Cominius. 'Twas from the canon [in excess of his
            authority].
Coriolanus.   'Shall'?
O good but most unwise patricians: why,
You grave but reckless senators, have you thus
Given Hydra here to choose an officer,
That with his peremptory 'shall'…
                wants not spirit
To say he'll turn your current in a ditch,
And make your channel his?

(3.1.88–96)

Power and status are here contested through a small word: 'shall'. Small in space but large in implication: note Coriolanus's adjectives for it: '*absolute* "shall"' and '*peremptory* "shall"'. It is an imperious verb, a commanding verb, one which encodes antagonistic power relations for 'as Coriolanus knows, there can only be one determiner of the "absolute": the word's very definition precludes plurality' (Kolentsis, 146). We recall that '*will* and *shall* best fitteth Tamburlaine', Marlowe's tyrannical invader and ruler (*1 Tamburlaine* 3.3.41).

LANGUAGE AND BOUNDARIES   **153**

'Modal' means 'relating to mood'; hence Tamburlaine's line above actually begins, 'Speak in that mood / For *will* and *shall* best fitteth Tamburlaine'. The mood expressed by modal verbs is that of possibility. The Elizabethan term for these verbs was the 'potential mood', a term first introduced into English by the humanist scholar and physician Thomas Linacre (1460–1524) and familiar to Shakespeare from Colet and Lily's *Grammar* (Magnusson, 71–2). Today we are less finely attuned to the distinctions between modals, or to the social implications of their use, than was Coriolanus; but his extreme reaction to the incendiary use of 'shall' should alert us to the importance of these verbs in the Elizabethan period.

Although these verbs are grouped together as 'modal', it is obvious that they subdivide and even polarize in both use and in meaning. Possibility in the verb 'can' can be expressed in dynamic, deontic or epistemic senses. Dynamic refers to an innate ability in the speaker where 'I can' means 'I am able' (I can dance a galliard). The deontic 'can' (from deontology: duty, moral or ethical obligation, from the Greek *deon*, *deont* – that which is binding) denotes permission as in 'you can park/smoke here': you are allowed to park/smoke here. Epistemic 'can' indicates possibility, as in 'There can be jealousy when …' Thus, there are subdivisions of use within modal verbs. And across the category we can see huge differences in modal meaning: for instance uncertainty and necessity are almost polar opposites.

Modal verbs are a fruitful category for examination in Elizabethan drama. Lynne Magnusson spells out their appeal:

People and playwrights are able to stage conflicts or negotiations within and between themselves over uncertain futures, calling up a complex array of competing drives. What is brought into play is not just warring passions but the fine-tuned and culturally inflected estimations of ability, obligation, volition and knowledge as they relate to future actions, conflicts and negotiations in which we can recognize the mind in motion: a psychology in the potential mood.

(Magnusson, 79)

The potential mood essentially defines drama, a world of possibilities. (As we saw in Chapter 2, 'Is't possible' is repeated five times in *Othello*.)

Modals invite wordplay (as seen above in *Coriolanus*) and offer overlaps in meaning as the dynamic, deontic and epistemic shade into each other (Magnusson 70). They thus work in much the same way that I have been arguing the pun does in this play – as a five-act dramatization of competing claims on meaning. Given that they 'foreground ... a speaker's stance in relation to knowledge' or serve as 'pivots for one or more speakers' competing interpretations' (Magnusson, 70), they open up a world of possibility.

Modals and power struggles in Marlowe

The drama of the 1590s is particularly focused on conflicts expressed in modals. Consider Marlowe's *Doctor Faustus*. In the first published text, in 1604, the Good Angel tells the hero/us:

Never too late, if Faustus can repent.

(2.3.79)

The revised text published in 1616 prints the line as follows:

Never too late, if Faustus will repent.

(2.3.80)

The distinction is partly theological (Calvinist predestination versus free will) but theology was being challenged by modal verbs as the humanist emphasis of the Renaissance split God's will from man's will. The deontic was no longer singularly God-given.

The Marlowe play in which modals structure the drama is *Edward II*. Critics have long noted a change in Marlovian rhetoric here. This is a play of dialogue, not of a protagonist's verbal power or monologue: Marlowe is writing for *voices*. It is a play in which the hero is not dominant (Edward II is hardly the hero of his own play.) It is also a play that lacks Marlowe's trademark 'mighty line'. The question is whether we see this as a development or as a loss ('oh what a falling off was there ...'; *Hamlet* 1.5.47).

A brief look at the following examples from Act One of *Edward II* may help us answer that question:

I **will** have Gaveston; and you **shall** know
What danger 'tis to stand against your King.

(1.1.95–6)

I **cannot** nor I **will** not; I **must** speak.

(1.1.121)

– So **will** I now and thou **shalt** back to France.
– Saving your reverence, you **must** pardon me.

(1.1.185)

We **may** not, nor we **will** not, suffer this.

(1.2.15)

And war **must** be the means, or he'**ll** stay still.

(1.2.63)

– What we confirm, the king **will** frustrate.

– Then **may** we lawfully revolt from him.

(1.2.72–3)

Ay, if words **will** serve; if not, I **must**.

(1.2.83)

This is a play about the power of will(s). And the power struggle is being fought out in modals.

Modals and power struggles in *Othello*

When Shakespeare writes *Othello* in 1604 (or, possibly, according to Honigmann, 1601–2) modals are being handled subtly. 'May' in the play's vocabulary expresses possibility (and therefore plurality). It is used this way, conventionally, correctly, grammatically, by all characters:

However this may gall him with some check

(1.1.146, Iago)

Do you know
Where we may apprehend her and the Moor?

(1.1.175, Brabantio)

My demerits
May speak unbonneted

(1.1.23, Othello)

Something from Cyprus, as I may divine

(1.2.39, Cassio)

So may he with more facile question bear it

(1.2.23, 1 Senator)

So much I challenge that I may profess

> (1.2.188, Desdemona)

As a grise or step may help these lovers

> (1.3.201, Duke)

'Shall' closes down plurality, offering compulsion. Again, the play's characters use this modal frequently and correctly. In the first Act alone:

you shall surely find him

> (1.1.154, Iago)

My services ... shall out-tongue his complaints

> (1.2.19, Othello)

Bond-slaves and pagans shall our statesmen be

> (1.2.98, Brabantio)

> The bloody book of law
> You shall yourself read, in the bitter letter

> (1.3.68–9, Duke)

And I a heavy interim shall support
By his dear absence

> (1.3.259–60, Desdemona)

As Aleksandra Thostrup observes, Iago's tactic, linguistic and ideational, is to slip the semantic glove of 'shall' onto 'may' and 'will' so that things become unidirectional, univocal, a question of absolute necessity. This begins in Act One when Iago presents the possibility of Othello and Desdemona growing bored with each other as a modal certainty:

It was a violent commencement in her, and thou *shalt* see an answerable sequestration [equal cessation]... The food that to him now is as luscious as locusts *shall* be to him shortly as acerb as coloquintida. She *must* change for youth ... she *must* have change, she *must*.

(1.3.344–52)

In Act Two he indulges in slippage: 'And nothing can or shall content my soul / Till I am evened with him, wife for wife' (2.1.296–7). The coordinating conjunction 'or', used normally to balance two equal elements of a sentence, here presents the modals as equal although 'can' is not as compulsive as 'shall'. In Iago's mouth, the epistemic 'can' slides into the compulsive 'shall'.

We hear this shift again in the long temptation scene of Act Three. Iago's 'this may help to thicken other proofs' has more certainty than possibility about its apparently innocent modal (3.3.432), as we see from Othello's preceding comment that 'this denoted a foregone conclusion'. Similarly, Iago's hesitant 'she may be honest yet' (3.3.436) uses a modal of possibility not to indicate plural options but to insinuate doubt about such an eventuality. The psychology of negation that we looked at in Chapter 2 (where cancelling a suggestion raises the possibility that it might be true) maps on to modal verbs. By Act Four, Iago is brazenly making inappropriate modal choices:

knowing what I am, I know what she shall be.

(4.173)

(An aside: this is another of his plays with 'to be'.) A paraphrase might run: 'knowing that I am an imperfect creature, I know that she is bound to be unchaste'. But an equally appropriate (less cynical) contrast would be with the modal 'may': 'I know what she *may* be'. And that this is the logical contrast may be seen from Shakespeare's use of a similar sentence in *Hamlet* when Ophelia says, 'we know what we are, but know not what we may be' (4.5.43–4). Ophelia's phrasing keeps ontological options open; Iago's closes them down, offering premature certainty. In this tactic, Iago knows his man. Othello does not 'do' uncertainty. 'To be once in doubt / Is once to be resolved' (3.3.182–3).

As we saw above, Susan Snyder has articulated the distinction between the comic and tragic worlds as one of evitability (in comedy) versus inevitability (in tragedy). This distinction – or, in *Othello*, morphology, whereby comedy becomes tragedy – is reflected in the play's language at the level of the modal auxiliary. Gradations of permission, possibility, predictability and necessity merge; or they are made to seem black-and-white rather than grey; and finally they switch places when mere possibility is seen as compulsion. The tragedy of *Othello* traces Othello's cumulative incapacity to distinguish between possibility and inevitability.

Iago's modal manipulations push the play from comedic evitability into tragic inevitability. We are used to foregrounding this generic change in action but it is also signalled by linguistic keywords, as we saw in Chapter 2. 'Is't possible' is a generic question. The entire play is in the potential mood. And when Matti Rissanen writes 'modals indicate either human control over or human judgment of future events' we see Iago wresting that control from Othello's use and meaning of modals to Iago's own (Rissanen, 231).

Modals and counterfactuals

Past tense forms of modals are often used in counterfactual conditional sentences with a *protasis* (a hypothetical introductory 'if' clause) and an *apodosis* (the consequent 'then' clause, where 'then' may be stated or implied). Iago's riddling ambiguities follow this form, as befits one whose forte is modal manipulation: 'Were I the Moor, I would not be Iago'

(1.1.56). In fact, counterfactual clauses are part of Iago's linguistic identity:

> If ever I did dream
> Of such a matter, abhor me.

$$(1.1.4-5)$$

> If the balance of our lives had not one scale of reason to pose another of sensuality, the blood and baseness of our natures would conduct us to most preposterous conclusions.

$$(1.3.327-30)$$

(This statement proves ironic as Iago manipulates Othello's lack of reason towards preposterous conclusions.)

> I mine own gained knowledge should profane
> If I would time expend with such a snipe.

$$(1.3.383-4)$$

> If such tricks as these strip you out of your lieutenantry, it had been better you had not kissed your three fingers so oft.

$$(2.1.171-3)$$

> If she had been blest she would never have loved the Moor.

$$(2.1.250-1)$$

The world of counterfactuals is not just for Iago a linguistic entity: he translates it into actuality, convincing Othello to believe in a hypothetical world. He makes the conditional counterfactual proposition come true, creating the world of the play. The counterfactual is Iago's medium, the medium of the plot. When other characters use counterfactual structures it is to try to *undo* the world of the play. Hearing about the handkerchief's magical properties, Desdemona says, 'would to

God that I had never seen't!' (3.4.79). Meditating on Othello's violence, Emilia tells her mistress, 'Would you had never seen him!' (4.3.16). Unsurprisingly, Othello's use of the counterfactual is lyrical, operatic, imaginative, unconfined by and unrelated to its own grammatical structure. In his reunion with Desdemona he makes two consecutive counterfactual statements:

> If after every tempest comes such calms
> May the winds blow till they have wakened death ...
> If it were now to die
> 'Twere now to be most happy.

> (2.1.183–8)

Here the hypothetical catastrophes are used hyperbolically to underline present happiness.

Ventriloquism

In Chapter 1 we looked at the way that Iago speaks a different language, one not understood by Roderigo or Cassio or Montano. In the examples we looked at, Iago's language does not infect either Roderigo or Cassio. However, its effect on Othello is clear and immediate. Iago puts words in Othello's mouth, almost literally ('O God, that men should put an enemy in their mouths, to steal away their brains!'; 2.3.285–7). In the scene in which Iago first plants suspicions in Othello's mind, he does so simply by echoing:

Othello.	Is he [Cassio] not honest?
Iago.	Honest, my lord?
Othello.	Honest? Ay, honest.
Iago.	My lord, for aught I know.
Othello.	What dost thou think?
Iago.	Think, my lord?

Othello.   Think, my lord! By heaven, thou echo'st me.

(3.3.103–9)

By Act Four, the linguistic positions are reversed. Scene 1 begins as follows:

Iago.   Will you think so?
Othello.   Think so, Iago?
Iago.   What,
              To kiss in private?
Othello.   An unauthorized kiss!
Iago.   Or to be naked with her friend in bed
              An hour or more, not meaning any harm?
Othello.   Naked in bed, Iago, and not mean harm?

(4.1.1–5)

Now it is Othello who is echoing Iago. A. D. Nuttall writes, 'Iago is so close to the Moor's ear, has insinuated himself so deeply into Othello's very thoughts, that one can hardly tell which speaker says which words' (Nuttall, 280). The play's anxiety about the border between Self and Other being an indistinct boundary is reified in language.

If we return to the play's opening scene, we can see how this linguistic blurring is foreshadowed. Simply put, Iago ventriloquizes other men.

The play's keywords are first used by Iago. Readers and audiences note the extreme linguistic breakdown of Othello in 4.1 when he exits having struck Desdemona: 'Goats and monkeys!' (4.1.263). We should also note that these nouns are first used by Iago in a series of similes; Othello's shorthand reference in Act Four is a remembrance of his ensign's earlier description when, faced with the task of providing 'ocular proof' of Desdemona's infidelity with Cassio, Iago says

It is impossible you should see this
Were they as prime as goats, as hot as monkeys,

As salt as wolves in pride.

(3.3.405–7)

When Iago uses the adjective 'salt' (lascivious) here it is his second use of the word; he applied it to Cassio's sexual disposition in Act Two, describing his 'salt and most hidden loose affection' (2.1.239). But Othello's use of the word in Act Three claims a different meaning: 'I have a salt and sullen rheum offends me, / Lend me thy handkerchief' (3.4.51–2). Here 'salt' means stinging or vexatious, and the handkerchief is associated with relief for eye-watering. But Iago twice limits the word's meaning to 'lascivious' and turns the handkerchief associated with it into proof of lasciviousness rather than relief for tears.

Othello's first words in the play are actually spoken by Iago: 'For "Certes," says he, / "I have already chose my officer"' (1.1.15–16). Of course, this is reported speech; but it establishes Iago's verbal technique and the pattern of the play in which Iago echoes Othello then Othello echoes him then finally Othello speaks with Iago's vocabulary.

In the 1989 RSC production, Ian McKellen's Iago not only quoted Othello here but imitated his accent. So too did the Johannesburg Market Theatre production (1988), carrying the imitation to even more reductive parody where Iago also reproduced Othello's gestures, including picking his nose (an additional invention by Iago, one presumes). It is worth exploring the scene's ventriloquistic aspects, concentrated (in text and in production) in the segment when Brabantio appears. Brabantio has been awakened by Roderigo at Iago's request: 'Call up her father / Rouse him ...' (1.1.66–7). Iago here directs Roderigo (who agrees: 'I'll call aloud'; 1.1.73) whereupon Iago provides a further directorial note: 'Do, with like timorous accent and dire yell' (1.1.74) ('Accent' in Shakespeare does not have its modern meaning of regional speech but refers to a branch of the classical rules of rhetoric, *pronuntiatio*, a way of speaking to create an emotional effect in an auditor; here the desired effect is fear. On accent in early modern England, see Jonathan Hope, *Shakespeare and Language*, 99–121.)

Productions differ in the staging of what follows. The dialogue is clear: Roderigo calls ('What ho!'; 1.1.77) and Iago supplements his call ('Awake, what ho, Brabantio!'; 1.1.78). When Brabantio appears, Roderigo asks if his family is within. Iago again reinforces Roderigo: 'Are your doors locked?' (1.1.84. This reintroduces the concept of his earlier supplementary questions where he twice referred to thieves.) Iago responds to Brabantio's question, 'Why? Wherefore ask you this?' (1.1.84) with his salacious metaphor about black rams and white ewes (1.1.87–8).

In the Trevor Nunn production, Roderigo (Michael Grandage) is shocked by Iago's vocabulary (he tells him 'shhh'). By contrast, in the 1964 National Theatre production (with Laurence Olivier and Maggie Smith) Michael Rothwell's Roderigo displays an amazed relish at Iago's linguistic daring and metaphoric imagination.

Roderigo's simple declaration, 'Most grave Brabantio, / In simple and pure soul I come to you' (1.1.105–6) can be a complete sentence: there is a full stop in both Quarto and Folio. (The full stop is adopted by editions in the Complete Works of the Royal Shakespeare Company, Norton and Oxford series.) Or the declaration can be interrupted by Iago (as it is in the punctuation in Honigmann's edition). Either way Iago's supplement changes the terms from purity and simplicity to sex and profanity:

> *Iago.*   Zounds, sir, you are one of those that will
> not serve God, if the devil bid you. Because
> we come to do you service, and you think
> we are ruffians, you'll have your daughter
> covered with a Barbary horse; you'll have your
> nephews neigh to you, you'll have coursers for
> cousins and jennets for germans!'
>
>   (1.1.107–12)

The BBC TV production makes much of the contrast between Roderigo's decorous speech to Brabantio and Iago's bawdy as two distinctive lexicons.

Brabantio's 'Thou art a villain' meets with a response from Iago that challenges readers today (and perhaps did so in the 1600s): 'You are a senator'. 'Senator' is possibly an insult (Honigmann explains it as a class insult, 1.1.116n). It may be a substitute term for the insult Iago was actually intending to hurl, before thinking better of it; the noun can therefore be preceded by a pause before a neutral, factual, deferential term: 'You are a — senator'. In the BBC TV production Roderigo is now at the height of his linguistic tolerance and ducks Iago's head in a nearby water butt, completing Iago's line with 'a senator' as a corrective and a rebuke to Iago for the bawdy insult he was clearly about to utter.

The productions cited above show the extent to which this is Iago's scene, linguistically. Nuttall's comment about dialogue in Act Four applies here too: it is hard to know who is speaking (Nuttall, 280). Productions which stage ventriloquism make this dynamic clear. In the 1964 National Theatre production, Iago hides behind Roderigo so the bawdy seems to come from Roderigo's mouth; the same happens in Oliver Parker's 1995 film where Iago hides behind Roderigo when he speaks.

In this opening scene Iago takes over Roderigo's language just as he later infects Othello's. (This is part of a larger use Iago has for Roderigo where, as we saw in Chapter 2, Roderigo provides a kind of rehearsal ground for Iago, his first gull.) We should recall that the English translation of the rhetorical figure of hendiadys is 'two in one' – a phrase which equally describes the play's/Iago's ventriloquism.

Tony Tanner extends the point about Iago's linguistic infection. He notes that Iago not only introduces blood into Othello's vocabulary but turns him into a man of blood. As 'an important servant and protector of the state [Othello] should be an instrument of law'; Iago 'introduces blood into his mind and discourse until they are both awash with the word' (Tanner 2010, 517):

My blood begins my safer guides to rule.

(2.3.201)

O, blood, blood, blood!

(3.3.454)

Even so my bloody thoughts with violent pace,
Shall ne'er look back, ne'er ebb to humble love.

(3.3.460–1)

I will be found most cunning in my patience;
But – dost thou hear? – most bloody.

(4.1.91–2)

Thy bed, lust-stained, shall with lust's blood be spotted.

(5.1.36)

Tanner continues: 'Yet Othello manages to convince himself, or allows Iago to manage this managing, that he is, throughout, administering "justice"' (Tanner 2010, 518). Iago's manipulation of language is also a manipulation of ideas and attitudes. In Act One the Duke had promised Othello 'the bloody book of law' (1.3.68). Iago turns this from a metaphor into a reality. His tactics are not simply linguistic: he is aware that language is who we are, not something appliquéd externally onto a separate interiority. The Ben Jonson quotation that I cited above continues as follows: 'language most shows a man: speak that I may see thee' (Hereford and Simpsons, 8:625). Once Othello starts to speak blood, he becomes a bloody man.

Prose and verse: Othello

So far in this chapter we have been looking at small units. I want now to move to the other extreme, from small words to a cumulative effect. Here, the two items I want to explore are prose and verse. As a rhetorician, as the composer and performer of the Othello music, Othello speaks in verse. Let us look at a few examples.

In several chapters we have mentioned Othello's speech to the Senate (and, in this chapter, noted its high proportion of hendiadys) in Act 1, scene 3. It is a speech typical of Othello's language and character (before Iago gets to work): balanced. Othello uses triadic structures: 'her father loved me, oft invited me, / Still questioned me' (1.3.129–30); he relates the 'battles, sieges, fortunes / That I have passed' (1.3.131–2). Note the three preterites: 'I *did* consent, / And often *did* beguile her of her tears / When I *did* speak' (1.3.156–58). He uses repetitive, anaphoric structures (*anaphora* is the repetition of the same word or phrase at the beginning of consecutive clauses or sentences): '*Of* moving accidents … / *Of* hair-breadth scapes … / *Of* being taken …/ *of* my redemption thence' (1.3.136–9). The repetition is hypnotic. And nothing in this speech is predictable: for instance, Othello reverses structures: 'This to hear / Would Desdemona seriously incline' (1.3.146–7).

We hear similar balanced construction, with the addition of sublimity, in his greeting to Desdemona when they are reunited in Cyprus:

> It gives me wonder great as my content
> To see you here before me! O my *soul's* joy,
> *If* after every tempest come such calms
> May the winds blow till they have wakened death,
> And let the laboring bark climb hills of seas,
> Olympus-high, and duck again as low
> As hell's from heaven. *If* it were now to die,
> 'Twere now to be most happy, for, I fear,

> My *soul* hath her content so absolute
> That not another comfort like to this
> Succeeds in unknown fate.
>
> (2.1.181–91, my italics)

The first line has a beautifully balanced simile. His address to Desdemona begins with a reference to his soul; the speech ends in the same way. Inside these bookends are two sentences beginning with 'if'. My italics indicate the chiastic structure: soul/if; if/soul.

By the time we get to Act 3, scene 3, Iago's poison has started to work. Othello talks of revenge. Iago counsels patience, as Othello may change his mind. Othello's response:

> Never, Iago. Like to the Pontic sea,
> Whose icy current and compulsive course
> Ne'er keeps retiring ebb, but keeps due on
> To the Propontic and the Hellespont:
> Even so my bloody thoughts, with violent pace,
> Shall ne'er look back, ne'er ebb to humble love,
> Till that a capable and wide revenge
> Swallow them up.
>
> (3.3.456–63; this speech is only in the Folio text)

This quotation is basically one sentence, one long image. It is still recognizable as Othello's vocabulary and syntax; it has a gathering of momentum; it is operatic. It uses incremental repetition ('never'/'ne'er' occurs four times). It still has the Othello music.

The actor Richard McCabe identifies Act Four as the place where 'Othello's language loses much of its heroic grandeur and is replaced by the more prosaic use of Iago's bestial imagery' (McCabe, 206). Consider the extraordinary change in 4.1.35–43: before Othello falls into an epileptic fit, he falls into prose. The prose is not even in sentences: 'Noses, ears, and lips'. Its logic is inverted: 'First to be hanged, and then to confess'. And its vocabulary is polluted by Iago's: Othello's 'Pish!' is a word first used by Iago to Roderigo on the quayside in Cyprus to dismiss the possibility of Desdemona being faithful (2.1.261).

When Othello returns to verse in the next scene it is now as disordered as his prose:

> Had it pleased heaven
> To try me with affliction, had they rained
> All kinds of sores and shames on my bare head,
> Steeped me in poverty to the very lips,
> Given to captivity me and my utmost hopes,
> I should have found in some place of my soul
> A drop of patience; but, alas, to make me
> A fixed figure for the time of scorn
> To point his slow and moving finger at!
> Yet could I bear that too, well, very well:
> But there, where I have garnered up my heart,
> Where either I must live, or bear no life,
> The fountain from the which my current runs,
> Or else dries up – to be discarded thence!
> Or keep it as a cistern for foul toads
> To knot and gender in! Turn thy complexion there,
> Patience, thou young and rose-lipped cherubin,
> Ay, here, look grim as hell!

(4.2.48–65)

The most detailed and subtle analysis of this comes from the critic Graham Bradshaw. He notes that the first half of the speech gives the impression of coherence with its series of liquid metaphors. Then it changes direction. Or rather, it does not change direction (which speeches are entitled to do) but combines the liquid metaphors with 'the very different idea of garnering or storing' (Bradshaw 2010, 80). This leads to contradictions in the speech's act of valuing: on the one hand, the garnering images show the value Othello has given

Desdemona – 'he has garnered up his heart by making her his storehouse of value' – but the liquid images show that her value 'exists as something objective, quite separate to him. She is now the "fountain" or source from which his own life derives significance or value' (Bradshaw 2010, 82–3).

The speech is complex and Bradshaw's brilliant analysis of it lengthy. You can find his analysis in two places. It occurs as an article in a Japanese journal, *Shakespeare Studies*, published in 2000. This article can be difficult to access but the material recurs in an abbreviated summary form (with a helpful spatial diagram of the speech's construction) on page 81 of Bradshaw's book on *Othello*, written for students. Bradshaw concludes 'The agony of confronting what cannot be endured produces a breakdown that is terrifyingly complete because it is syntactic and logical, as well as emotional and psychological' (Bradshaw 2010, 80). Kenneth Gross concludes that 'it is as if [Othello's] desire to tear his wife "all to pieces" [3.3.434] or "chop her into messes" [4.1.197] returns upon his speech with a vengeance' (Gross, 829).

Prose and verse: Iago

Iago by contrast is at home in both prose and verse; he is formally bilingual. But prose is his most fluid medium. Here is an example from Act Two when he observes Cassio welcoming Desdemona on the quayside in Cyprus:

(1) He takes her by the palm; (2) ay, well said, whisper. (3) With as little a web as this will I ensnare as great a fly as Cassio. (4) Ay, smile upon her, do: (5) I will gyve [fetter] thee in thine own courtesies. (6) You say true, 'tis so, indeed. (7) If such tricks as these strip you out of your lieutenantry, it had been better you had not kissed your three fingers so oft, (8) which now again you are most apt to play the sir in. (9) Very good, well kissed, and excellent

courtesy: (10) 'tis so, indeed! (11) Yet again your fingers to your lips? (12) would they were clyster-pipes for your sake!

(2.1.167–77).

Our guide to the careful construction of this speech is Alessandro Serpieri, who numbers each part of the sequence for analysis as I have done (Serpieri, 137). Something is happening on stage (courtesies between Cassio and Desdemona) and Iago is observing what happens: he comments on the action to us and also (unheard) to Cassio. The overall arc of the speech is thus a contrast between 'I' and 'you'. But this simple binary becomes a triad: the 'I' of Iago addresses the unhearing 'you' of Cassio but when he talks about 'he' he is addressing a third party, us, the audience.

If we follow the numerical sequence, we can see how it works. (1) describes the action; (2) encourages Cassio; (3) distances Cassio and involves us, the audience; (4) encourages the 'you' to implicate him; (5) addresses the 'you' again but foregrounds 'the predatory function of the "I"'; (6) offers ironic commentary; (7) changes the threat of (3) to direct address; (8) brings Iago close to the action again; (9) offers commentary on the action, cynical and detached; (10) in anticipation underlines (11); (11) also feigns surprise at the repeated action; (12) attacks the 'you' in 'an anal fantasy that transforms the courteous scene – already changed into an erotic scene – into a perverse exchange' (Serpieri, 137–8). From this dazzling performance in prose we can understand why Frank Kermode finds Iago 'least interesting when he is thinking in verse' (Kermode, 173).

Theatre boundaries

I want to consider one final boundary – the boundary between fact and fiction, between real life and theatre. This takes us back to the relation between speaker and auditor in story-telling (Chapter 1), the boundaries of genre (Chapter 2) and boundaries in language (this chapter). Let us now see how all these boundaries interact in relation to drama; or rather, let us look at the play as an exploration of dramatic boundaries.

When Desdemona listens to tales of Othello's adventures and responds with pity and love, we are reminded of the obvious classical precursor for the episode: Aeneas' narration of the fall of Troy, which affects Dido similarly. Aeneas' narrative and the ensuing love affair spans two books in Virgil's *Aeneid*; it is given dramatic form in Marlowe and Nashe's *Dido, Queen of Carthage* (c. 1588), a play which Shakespeare recalls in *Hamlet*. In Marlowe and Nashe's play, Dido entreats Aeneas to 'discourse at large, / And truly too, how Troy was overcome' (2.1.106–7). Aeneas responds with the longest speech in the play (lines 121–288) – an unusual tour de force for a boy actor (whose speeches are usually much shorter). The speech is punctuated only by four one-line inter-ruptions from Aeneas' auditors with expressions of emotion or petitions for him to continue.

Like Aeneas, and like other military adventurers who have (and subsequently recount) strange experiences of strange peoples in strange lands, who move others by their exploits, appearance and rhetoric, Othello is an epic hero. Critics have long noted that Othello's identity in his autobiographical tale to Desdemona, like all identity, is performative, a rhetorical construct, projected, packaged, displayed, and that his sense of himself is dependent on his audience's response. This is the idea we find in *Julius Caesar* where Brutus says 'the eye sees not itself / But by reflection' (*Julius Caesar* 1.2.52–3) and in *Troilus and Cressida* where Ulysses says that no man knows his qualities 'Till he behold them formed in th' applause' (3.3.119). In *Othello* this leads to the question of traditional character criticism: can Desdemona really know Othello or he her, given that what he presents and she responds to is a performance? When Othello summarizes his courtship – 'She loved me for the dangers I had passed / And I loved her that she did pity them' (1.3.168–9), Honigmann ponders in a footnote, 'How well does he understand her love, or his own?' Or to rephrase his implied anxiety in narrative and theatrical terms, the problem is that Desdemona blurs the storyteller and the story told; she confuses the character and the actor.

Crossing theatre boundaries

For a situation which both parallels and contrasts Desdemona's, a situation in which the domestic female falls in love with the theatrical leading man, we need (at the risk of absurdity) to fast forward to the twentieth century and enter the world of film. This, in fact, is what Mia Farrow's character, Cecilia, does in Woody Allen's *The Purple Rose of Cairo* (1985), set in the 1930s. Having lost her job, Cecilia escapes dullness and dangerous domestic abuse by spending her time at the cinema. One day, after a particularly ugly marital episode, she retreats to round-the-clock screenings of *The Purple Rose of Cairo*. Her repeat viewings and emotional response catch the attention of the film's hero, Tom Baxter, who addresses her from the screen, eventually leaving the screen to woo her in impoverished Depression-era New Jersey. With considerably more self-awareness than Desdemona, Cecilia analyses her predicament: 'I met a perfect man today. He's fictional; but you can't have everything'.

For an Elizabethan version of this metatheatrical triangle we might turn to the diary of the law student, John Manningham. While he was a student at the Middle Temple, Manningham kept a diary that covers the year(s) 1602–3. Part diary, part commonplace book, his compilation from London life includes the following anecdote:

> Upon a time when Burbage played Richard III there was a citizen grown so far in liking with him, that before she went from the play she appointed him to come that night unto her by the name of Richard the Third. Shakespeare overhearing

their conclusion went before, was entertained and at his game ere Burbage came. Then message being brought that Richard the Third was at the door, Shakespeare caused return to be made that William the Conqueror was before Richard the Third.

(Manningham, 39; I have modernized the spelling)

The story is famous for its onomastic joke (obligingly underlined by Manningham's concluding explanation: 'Shakespeare's name, William') and its comic sexual punch line. But like the stories of Dido and Aeneas, of Desdemona and Othello, of Cecilia and Tom, the (possibly apocryphal) story of the female citizen and Burbage/Richard III raises questions about the boundaries between fictional characters and real-life characters. When Desdemona crosses the boundary between audience and stage to marry the actor-hero, she initiates a tragedy of theatre boundaries gone wrong.

Boundaries gone wrong

Othello's vocabulary is self-consciously theatrical from the beginning as we saw in the case of Iago as a playwright figure and director; but we also saw it linguistically in the way in which character's identities become confused as they speak each other's lines, words, phrases. This is a violation of theatrical rules: identity in the theatre is rhetorically constructed. We know who characters are because of the way they speak like themselves (see the work of Altmann, Melchiori, Holland, Calderwood in the bibliography).

The things that go wrong in this play have theatrical (or metatheatrical) valence. Characters have premature entrances. Desdemona arrives in Cyprus seven days before she's expected (contrast the play's source in Cinthio, where all the characters arrive together because they have travelled on the same boat). Bianca enters in Act Four, not on cue, to berate Cassio. Cassio's first words to her are: 'What do you mean by this haunting of me?' (4.2.147) – in other words, 'What are you doing here? I wasn't expecting you'. In several stage and film versions, Roderigo's entrances are unexpected and take Iago by surprise; the direction gives the strong feeling that Roderigo should not be there and Iago is driven to improvise. At the end of the Senate scene, Kenneth Branagh's Iago (director Oliver Parker, 1995) turned to the camera, clearly on the verge of a soliloquy, only to be prevented by Roderigo ('Iago!'; 1.3.302). The same happened again, after Iago's soliloquy, in 2.3: Iago was taken off guard by Roderigo's entrance ('How now, Roderigo?'; 2.3.357). This was also true of the BBC film throughout where Roderigo showed up to ask Iago awkward questions at awkward times. And even Desdemona gets lines out of sequence in the willow song, interrupting herself with the (self)directorial correction, 'Nay, that's not next' (4.3.52).

The characters are scripted as actors in a play: '*Othello* is a play that assigns parts with obsessive (if controversial) discursive particularity' (Rutter, 148). So too the plot (which is itself a plot of plots and improvisations) is insistently coded as theatrical. The gulling of Roderigo is a rehearsal for the gulling of Othello. Othello's voyeurism parallels our own as spectators. Both Desdemona and Roderigo speak after they've technically been pronounced dead: Desdemona revives (impossibly) after being strangled; Roderigo 'spake / (After long seeming dead)' (5.2.327–8). These are both physiological miracles and amateur dramatic errors. Commenting on Trevor Nunn's production of the play, Carol Rutter notes Emilia's horror as she watches Desdemona's story move into domestic tragedy:

Emilia was watching a *story* – one she knew familiarly, a story of domestic abuse. Confusingly to her, the narrative wasn't where she'd left it, but rather displaced, shifted from one house-hold onto another, so that Othello was playing Iago's part and, uncannily, Desdemona her abject self.

(Rutter 165–6)

Here a number of generic and theatrical boundaries are being crossed simultaneously.

Character motivation is also relevant to the play's theatrical tropes. *Othello* is, crucially, a play in which key actors have no motive. Iago's lack of motive is famous. But Othello also merits attention because of the way in which his speeches repeat nouns like 'cause' and 'motive' and because of his obsession with finding the causes of things: 'who began this?' (2.3.178). Critics and actors often ponder Emilia's motive for stealing the handkerchief. We associate motive with twentieth-century Method acting in which actors immerse themselves in their characters but recent research has shown how this is a crucial component of Elizabethan acting – whether you locate it, as Lorna Hutson and James McBain do, in the influence of legal rhetoric (whose purpose was to create or demolish the character of a defendant or witness) or, as Tiffany Stern and Simon Palfrey do, in the questions forced upon the Elizabethan actor who tried to construct his emotional and practical situation in a scene from incomplete knowledge: he received only his own part plus a one- to three-word cue. Thus, long before the twentieth century, motive is an important theatrical ingredient. Shakespeare removes this theatrical essential.

The play's theatre vocabulary also includes the spectator. One of the interesting things about spectatorship is the paradoxical nature of its interest in the actor-character: we want to interact with the hero – to be in his world, his life – but we also want to *be* the hero. Gender is not relevant: a female spectator can want to be the hero's wife and she can simultaneously want to be the hero himself. Desdemona's language registers this audience doubleness: she 'wish'd / That heaven had made her such a man' (1.3.162–3). Made a man like that for her (where 'her' is dative)? or created her as an action-hero (where 'her' is accusative)? The grammatical ambiguity registers perfectly the audience experience where the answer is: both.

When Desdemona crosses the boundary from audience to drama with her romantic interest in Othello she initiates a comic structure. Almost all the inductions or plays-within-plays which show spectators interacting with a player are comedies. It is customary to view *Othello* as a tragedy that begins as a comedy, as we saw in Chapter 2. The location of this comic opening is usually seen either in the elopement (a conventional comic plot) or the January-May marriage (conventional cuckold comedy). I think the generic problem begins when Desdemona can't keep audience and actor separate.

Once this theatrical boundary is crossed, every other theatrical boundary falls. *No-one* in this play understands genre. As we saw earlier, Desdemona's artless and loving repetitions when she petitions Othello for Cassio's reinstatement flout every conduct book rule for the dutiful wife and take her into the comic territory of the nagging shrew. The unfunny Clown is likewise a problem – he is generically wrong. So too Roderigo who, despite Iago casting him as a gull, sees himself as a romantic hero. The actor Richard McCabe says 'Roderigo is no fool but a young man in the throes of desperate infatuation' (McCabe, 194). The 2007 production at Shakespeare's Globe chose to emphasize Roderigo's own 'mini-tragedy' (the DVD extras provide interviews describing this process).

If the tragedy begins when/because Desdemona crosses the boundary between audience and play, it ends in the same way when Othello blurs the boundary between drama and life. Othello tells a story about what he did to someone in Aleppo and then identifies himself with that someone as he 'smote him – thus' (5.2.356). A grammatical third person becomes a physical first-person; 'him' in the narrative is now inseparable from 'myself' in the present. Othello resurrects the distancing boundaries of theatre only to cross them. And between Desdemona's theatrical boundary-crossing at the beginning and Othello's at the end, every other theatrical boundary falls: genre collapses, language collapses, identity collapses – and always in the same way: two separate things become one.

It is customary to view *Othello* as a play about Self and Other. I am suggesting here that it understands those categories as theatrical rather than (or as well as) racial: that the plot originates not in a white woman marrying a black man but in an audience member falling in love with an actor-character and crossing from the world of audience to the world of fiction.

As it happens, performance history offers more examples of audience interruption of *Othello* than of any other Shakespeare play. In 1660 Samuel Pepys tells how a lady near him cried out when Desdemona was smothered. In 1825 a man in the front row called Iago a 'damn'd lying scoundrel' and offered to meet him after the show to break his neck. In 1822 in Baltimore a soldier on guard duty in the theatre shot the actor of Othello saying 'It will never be said in my presence a confounded Negro has killed a white woman' (Hankey, 17, 4–5). Audience members, I suggest, are responding to the play's own confusion of boundaries.

Julie Hankey's production history of *Othello* notes the temptation for Iagos to upstage their Othellos (Hankey, 27); Othello may be the tragic hero but Iago has the longer role, more soliloquies, and direct addresses to the audience. Thus the thespian relationship between Othellos and Iagos starts to parallel the play's plot. Playing Othello in the eighteenth century, Samuel Foote was grateful that his Iago, Charles Macklin, 'understood his subordinate position' (the phrasing is Hankey's, 27). Iago is doubly kept in his place, subordinate as character and as actor: subordinate in the play to Cassio's lieutenancy, subordinate in the company because he's not the titular hero. Where is the boundary here between play world and real world?

Writing matters

1. Small words

Follow the progress of one of Iago's 'small words'. 'Yet' might make a good starting point. How does it join phrases or ideas? Is it always logical? Does Iago's use of the conjunction change across the play? Are there any examples where its use surprises you?

Now look at one of the *play*'s use of small words. 'Never' is a good example. The play begins and ends with 'never' in relation to two forms of Iago's silence: 'never tell me' in Act One, refers to Iago's past silence; 'from this time forth I never will speak word' in Act Five refers to his future silence. Iago uses it repeatedly in the Cyprus quayside scene: 'She never yet was foolish that was fair …' (2.1.136). Othello uses the adverb in Act Two when he dismisses Cassio: 'never more be officer of mine' (2.3.245). In pleading for reinstatement, is Cassio fighting against an adverbial finality that is encoded as tragic? Is Emilia fighting against something equally futile when she tries to rewrite history: 'Would you had never seen him' (4.3.17)? Does the play's tragic inevitability culminate in Act Five's repeated 'never'? Desdemona says: 'I never did / Offend you in my life, never loved Cassio / But with such general warranty of heaven / As I might love: I never gave him token' (5.2.58–61); 'I never gave it him' (5.267); Cassio says, 'I never gave you cause' (5.2.296). Or do these past tense uses function almost as counterfactuals? Does Iago's use of this word manipulate time schemes differently from other characters (just as he manipulates words and language differently)?

2. Modals

Let us look at three speeches in which Iago manipulates modals. Here is part of the speech in which Iago works on Roderigo in Act Two. One of my students has marked his modals and made marginal comments about their use, and about how they interact with his vocabulary:

...**will** she love him still for prating? let not thy discreet heart think it. Her eye **must** be fed, and what delight **shall** she have to look on the devil? ... Now, for want of these required conveniences, her delicate tenderness **will** find itself abused, begin to heave the gorge, disrelish and abhor the Moor; very nature **will** instruct her in it and compel her to some second choice. Now, sir, this granted – as it is a most pregnant and unforced position ...

[hypothetical 'will', but 'must'/'shall' deplete the language of possibility]

[assertive not hypothetical 'will']

['very nature' – the hermeneutic frame Iago erects]

(2.1.222–34)

Here is Iago speaking to Othello in Act Three. Again, my student has marked the modals and the other vocabulary with which they interact.

What then? how then?
What **shall** I say? where's
    satisfaction?
It is impossible you **should** see
    this,
Were they as prime as goats,
    as hot as monkeys,
As salt as wolves in pride, and
    fools as gross
As ignorance made drunk. But
    yet, I say,
If imputation and strong
    circumstances
Which lead directly to the
    door of truth,
Will give you satisfaction, you
    may have't.

[conjecture versus certitude]

[strategically placed 'if's/modals: line breaks and points of emphasis/pause, places where the voice 'turns' and makes the mind pivot in a hermeneutic labyrinth]

(3.3.404–11)

Here is part of Iago's third soliloquy:

> His soul is so enfetter'd to her love,
> That she **may** *make, unmake,* do what she list,
> Even as her appetite **shall** play the god
> With his weak function. How am I then a villain
> To counsel Cassio to this parallel course,
> Directly to his good? Divinity of hell!
> When devils **will** the blackest sins put on,
> They do suggest at first with heavenly shows,
> As I do now: for whiles this honest fool
> Plies Desdemona to repair his fortunes
> And she for him pleads strongly to the Moor,
> I'll pour this pestilence into his ear,
> That she repeals him for her body's lust;
> And by how much she strives to do him good,
> She **shall** undo her credit with the Moor.
> So **will** I turn her virtue into pitch,
> And out of her own goodness make the net
> That **shall** enmesh them all.

(2.3.340–57)

I have emphasized the modal verbs in bold. Can you annotate the speech with comments like those made in the margins above? Here are some suggestions to get you started: look at the change from the indeterminate permissive 'may' and the ongoing present of 'shall play the god' to the determined predetermined 'shall undo', 'that shall enmesh them all' (2.3.354; 357). And consider the collocation of 'make / unmake' in relation both to verbs in this speech and Iago's other verbs in the play.

3. Proverbs

Look back at the section on proverbs in Chapter 1. Proverbs

are an extended example of Iago's subtle use of small linguistic units in the play. Document the play's use of proverbs and use Chris Cannon's superb article, 'Proverbs and the Wisdom of Literature', to help you analyse them.

CHAPTER FOUR

Writing tips and topics

Writing an essay is your reward for having done all the hard work of thinking about the topic. Now you get the chance to put it all together, to write elegantly, to persuade someone else of your opinion … Enjoy it.

That makes it sound like your essay is just a conduit for finished thoughts. It may be: some writers know exactly what they are going to argue from beginning to end. But writing can also be an important part of the thinking process: elaborations or qualifications or counterarguments may come to you in the act of writing, suggested by the process itself. So make a plan but don't worry if you have to interrupt it.

I say 'interrupt', not 'abandon': think of your essay as a main road in which you are heading continuously in one direction but can take detours to smell the flowers, explore a historic monument, or take a B-road – but you never lose sight of your destination and always rejoin the main road.

Tips

1 Identify your subject in a forceful but succinct introduction. Essays which respond to a strong statement – '*Othello* is a play about racism', for example – are often easier to set up because the

bluntness of the quotation gives you something concrete to react to (whether by agreement or rejection).

Since essay questions are springboards for sophisticated thought it is important to avoid a literal answer. A question about the monstrous should not simply catalogue references to monsters. Think about how *Othello* uses this word; about the questions it raises about categorizing the Other; and about the issues it raises about what is natural/unnatural in early modern life and on stage (see below: 'The natural/unnatural'). Always consider where the question *leads*. Or to pick up the motorway analogy above: having driven from A to B, don't stop; think about what there might be to see at C; then push yourself on towards D; try to get as far as E. That way you have an essay that develops.

2   You don't need to go overboard on detail. Deft selection of references from representative scenes/episodes will give authority to your answer; examples from every episode will suggest you don't know how to extract the most salient points. On the other hand, don't skimp on detail. Your argument needs to be illustrated from the text; the text should always be the main focus of your answer. Don't ruin a potentially good essay by leaving your views unsupported.

3   An essay should contain analysis, not description, There is no point in retelling the plot. Obviously, some narrative will be unavoidable but dispense with it quickly and move to the point, which is interpretation.

4   Your essay should be a persuasive rhetorical unity not just a collection of miscellaneous thoughts. Motivate your paragraph links by thinking ahead; thus you can pave the way for the next topic by including a transition at the end of the previous paragraph.

5   There are no divisions between reading and writing.

Read in order to learn how to write. In whatever you read (academic books, articles, newspaper columns), notice not just what the author argues but how he or she argues it. In whatever you next write, try to imitate a style or technique that has impressed you. (Imitation is not plagiarism; imitation is the sincerest form of flattery.) Remember that a Shakespeare play is not the only text that requires your critical attention. Academic articles also need eagle-eyed analysis: do you agree with the argument? Why? How is the argument made? What assumptions does it make? Are there contradictions? Is its vocabulary manipulating you in a specific direction? Does it betray its own assumptions?

6 Lengthy essays and verbose sentences do not necessarily guarantee clear communication. (I think it was George Bernard Shaw who made the famous apology for writing a long letter because he did not have the time to write a short one. The sentiment is also attributed to Pascal, Voltaire and Mark Twain.) Practise being precise and succinct. Start with daily conversation: good speakers are usually good writers. Work on expanding your vocabulary. You can't have ideas until you have the words in which to think them. The wider your vocabulary, the more precise your writing will be.

7 Aristotle wrote that the incidents of plot 'must be so arranged that if any one of them is differently placed or taken away the effect of wholeness will be seriously disrupted. For if the presence or absence of something makes no apparent difference, it is no real part of the whole' (*Poetics*, Chapter 8). His comments are applicable to essays too. Ask yourself: is this necessary? What will happen if I rearrange this point? If I leave it out? Handwriting your first draft can help you here since Cut and Paste is not an option! When

you handwrite a paragraph you have to know what
the next paragraph will say and write towards it.
(Theoretically this should be true of word-processing
too but because it is so easy to change the order
round, it is tempting just to put something down on
screen and think about its relevance later.) Allow
yourself plenty of time for editing and ruthless cutting
and learn to be your own severest critic. It has been
said that there is no such thing as a good writer: there
are only good *re*-writers.

8   Don't use critics as a substitute for your own thinking
    and don't quote them at length. A brief phrase
    or sentence should suffice. Epitomize the critic's
    argument: you should qualify, develop or disagree
    with their case. The reader needs to know why the
    critic's quotation is there.

9   General introductions are irritating. Avoid offering
    a history of Elizabethan drama, the development
    of Shakespearean tragedy or bardolatrous praise of
    Shakespeare as a genius. Until you have done some
    close analysis, the reader has no idea if you actually
    know what you are talking about or if you are just
    waffling.
        Avoid generalization or unproven statements.
    By simple modification, a general statement can be
    converted into a pithy observation. Often it needs no
    more than a parenthetical observation or a judiciously
    chosen adjective to convert a generalized statement
    into a critical observation.
        Conclusions should add something, not just sum
    up what you have been saying. (Avoid statements like
    'Thus it can be seen that …'). I do not mean that a
    conclusion should add new information or introduce
    a new topic: that is definitely wrong in a conclusion.
    But it can add a new inflexion or a subtle twist to the
    material it is summarizing.

10 An essay is not a business report. Avoid writing
your essay in sections with headings like 'Theme',
'Structure', 'Character', 'Language' as if they are
separate elements. (As we have seen in this book,
everything is language and vice versa.) Section
headings can be helpful if they are very specific – go
back and look at the subheadings I have used in this
book and see what work they are doing or what help
they are providing. Section headings can also be useful
in organizing your drafts and keeping you on track as
they provide a summary reminder of what you should
be writing about.

This is also true of the smaller unit of the
paragraph: in your margin, add a one-word summary
of each paragraph. (If you can't do this, then your
paragraph doesn't have a focus.) Then remove these
tag-summaries at the end. Think of each paragraph as
a mini-essay with its own introduction, argument, and
conclusion.

11 Your essay needs to have fluidity. Avoid clunky
phrases like 'This essay will argue'; 'I will do …'; 'an
example of this is'. If you are arguing something, your
reader will see it without being told that this is what
is happening. (These phrases are helpful in lengthy
academic writing – book chapters, for instance – but
should not be necessary in essays of 2,000 words or
less.)

12 Note that I have called this section 'Tips': it is not
a blueprint. There is no blueprint for essay writing.
Different topics require different kinds of organization,
different kinds of introductions, different levels of
detail: practise organizing your material in a number
of ways. If your exam system gives you Assessment
Objectives, remember that they are there to guide
you and not to work as a Paint by Numbers formula.
Biographical information and context? Not all essays

need this. Similarly, comparisons between different
critics' views and approaches can be helpful, or not,
depending on your topic and argument.

Topics

Race

For us, *Othello* is the quintessential play about race. It may
not always have been seen this way. As a result, there are
many ways of approaching this topic.

- Jean Howard draws our attention to the popularity
  of adventure plays with Moors and Turks on the
  Elizabethan and Jacobean stage (Howard 2005, 90–9).
  Some of these plays depict interracial marriages. Some
  are based on true stories, others are fiction. It is worth
  looking at them to see what *Othello* does differently.
  (See George Peele's *The Battle of Alcazar* (c. 1589),
  the anonymous *Captain Thomas Stukeley* (1605),
  John Day, William Rowley and George Wilkins's *The
  Travels of Three English Brothers* (1607), Robert
  Daborne's *A Christian Turned Turk* (1612), among
  others.) Howard notes that these plays all show
  Englishmen going abroad, converting to Islam, being
  seduced by foreign women; the originality of *Othello*
  is to show this process from the other direction.
  Othello does not turn Turk: he turns Christian. The
  threat is not from a sexual black woman but a chaste
  white woman. Othello is not an adventuring white
  European but a black African. Here as elsewhere,
  Shakespeare looks with the eyes of the outsider.

- We might be able to link Howard's observation about
  adventure plays with the links between *Othello* and
  Tamburlaine we noted in Chapter 2. Tamburlaine's

conquests (which he summarizes at the end of *Part Two*) are from East to West. This is, obviously, the opposite of European imperialist ambition which saw the trajectory of conquest as being in the opposite direction. (Lisa Hopkins writes wonderfully about this in '"And shall I die, and this unconquered?": Tamburlaine's Inverted Colonialism'.) *Tamburlaine* is another play to add to Howard's list – a play that, as we have seen, already has important links to *Othello* in terms of genre. Do those links extend to race?

● It is helpful to investigate the instability of the term 'Moor' in Shakespeare's England. You can do this by looking at Moors in the plays listed above, in two other Shakespeare plays, *Titus Andronicus* and *The Merchant of Venice*, and by reading articles and books by Dympna Callaghan, Celia Daileader, Kim Hall, G. K. Hunter, Eldred Jones and Michael Neill (Neill, '"Mulattos", "Blacks" and "Indian Moors"'). For information about how Elizabethans portrayed Moors on stage, see Ian Smith's article and its conclusions.

● Production history is always helpful. In this instance, it leads to an important ideological question: should Othello be played by a white actor or a black actor? As recently as 1981 Anthony Hopkins played Othello in the BBC film in black face makeup, a process unthinkable today (it is called 'minstrel racism', referring to a popular 1960s television programme, *The Black and White Minstrel Show*.) However, the black actor Hugh Quarshie believes that a black actor playing Othello unwittingly endorses the play's stereotype that to be black is to be emotional; he says that being black gives an actor no more insight into playing Othello than being Danish does to the actor of Hamlet. Michael Neill traces the relation between *Othello* productions and the historical *Zeitgeist* as regards race relations (in separatist America, apartheid

South Africa, for instance) and asks 'when did
Othello become a tragedy of race?' He suggests that
Elizabethans might have been more disturbed by the
violation of class in the play (Neill, '"His Master's
Ass"' and '"Servile Ministers"').

● In thinking about race, we might ask why Shakespeare
put a plot about racism with a plot about jealousy.
Issues of motivation, and the anti-Moor history
implicit in Iago's name (see Introduction), come
into play here. Racism is an emotion that has no
motivation or basis in reason; as the English essayist
Sydney Smith (1771–1845) said of prejudice generally,
'Never try to reason the prejudice out of a man. It
was not reasoned into him.' In Act Four, Desdemona
tells Emilia that Othello has no cause to suspect
Desdemona of sexual infidelity. Emilia explains that

> Jealous souls will not be answered so:
> They are not ever jealous for the cause,
> But jealous for they're jealous. It is a monster
> Begot upon itself, born on itself.

> (3.4.159–62)

Jealousy and racism are parallel emotions, parallel
attitudes. Shakespeare is interested in exploring
causeless emotions. An essay on race in the play could
profitably include an inquiry into the play's treatment
of jealousy and consider the relevance of one to the
other.

Motivation

Motivation has been an issue for *Othello* critics ever since
Samuel Taylor Coleridge wrote the phrase 'the motive-hunting
of motiveless Malignancy' in the margin of his copy of the text
while he was preparing lectures on Shakespeare in 1819. The

problem, as critics realize, is not that Iago has no motive but that he has too many. As with the question of race there are several ways of approaching this topic.

- If you cite Coleridge, it is important to look at the context in which he used the phrase (start by reading his lecture in Foakes's edition, volume 2) – and also work out what he meant by 'motive'. He discusses the distinction between 'Motives and Impulses' in a short work published in 1812 (volume 1 in *Shorter Works and Fragments*).

- You can approach this topic via source study. Motivation is clear in Cinthio's novella, opaque in Shakespeare. Why?

- You can examine Iago's soliloquies and logic. Iago is very explicit about his tactic – to make the Moor jealous. But, as Alexander Leggatt observes, he is not so explicit about 'what he hopes to accomplish' (Leggatt 2005, 122). One question we have to ask ourselves is: what does Iago gain? Cassio's lieutenancy is one obvious answer. But why does Iago not stop what he is doing once he has been promoted to Cassio's place?

- W. H. Auden wrote that 'Since the ultimate goal of Iago is nothingness, he must not only destroy others but himself as well' (Auden, cited by Sher, 62). Iago is the great uncreator. Antony Sher made this the heart of his interpretation when he played Iago in 2004: 'Iago just seems to be on some nihilistic joyride' (Sher, 62). Sher played the couplet, 'This is the night / That either makes me or fordoes me quite' (5.1.128–9) as 'offering a buzz either way' (Sher, 62).

- Performance history is again helpful as we look at the motives that directors and actors have assigned to their interpretation. For instance, many productions suggest a gay Iago. (As we saw in Chapter 2, this is not especially helpful as motive – do gay men usually destroy heterosexual men?) The 2007 production at Shakespeare's Globe gave Iago a black wife, making the play a double tragic exploration of jealousy. When Iago cautions Othello against jealousy he describes the emotion in detail – is it because he knows whereof he speaks? (Antony Sher believes that the play is not about one jealous husband but two; Sher, 58). Giving Iago a black wife offered a character who was determined to make Othello experience the pain of suspicion he himself experienced – the pain of uncertainty that his wife might prefer someone of her own kind.

- Critics sometimes describe Iago as an allegorical figure, pure evil. How easy is it for an actor to play an abstraction rather than a man?

Women

Think about the way the play slanders all of the play's women as whores (look back at the Introduction and Chapter 2). Look at the evidence for and against each accusation. What do we make of a Cassio who deifies Desdemona on the quayside but dismisses and derogates Bianca? Are the play's stereotypes of women mapped onto its stereotypes of race?

The natural / unnatural

This is an issue that is coloured in the play by both Brabantio's prejudice ('For nature so preposterously to err ...'; 1.3.63) and by Iago's ('Not to affect many proposed matches / Of her own clime, complexion and degree, / Whereto we see, in all things, nature tends'; 3.3.233–5). It is an issue that is also explored outside the category of race: for instance, the play contrasts the 'natural' jealousy of Bianca with the Iago-manipulated jealousy of Othello.

I might be inclined to approach this topic by tracing a related word, 'monstrous'. Almost every Act of *Othello* foregrounds the word 'monster' or 'monstrous'. The first comes in Iago's soliloquy at the end of Act 1, scene 3, where in a perspicacious metaphor of himself as a perverted maternal creator, Iago registers the monstrous birth that he hopes will ensue (1.3.402–3). Act Two opens with the 'monstrous' tempest (2.1.13), followed by the 'monstrous' violation of decorum (2.3.213) when soldiers brawl on duty. In Act Three, Iago curses the 'monstrous' world where to 'be direct and honest is not safe' (3.3.380–1). In the same scene Othello characterizes Cassio's dream of Desdemona as 'monstrous! monstrous!' (3.3.428). In Act Five, when the murder of Desdemona is revealed, Montano's immediate reaction is 'O monstrous act!' (5.2.186). How is the word used in all these occurrences? Is it a consistent synonym for 'unnatural'?

Romance stories of women and monsters or monsters and heroes have a long history: Beauty and the Beast, Andromeda and Perseus. And it is not just women who are fascinated by monster stories: Brabantio invites and questions Othello ('oft'). Can we link the play's interest in the unnatural with its interest in story-telling? The monstrous is a key ingredient in romance narrative.

If the play investigates the unnatural, perhaps it does so not by staging a mixed marriage but by examining the agent who destroys that marriage. As Wes Williams points out, 'the monster is not, finally, an object of knowledge so much as a question asked of systems of representation, a question that concerns our understanding of what it means to be human' (Williams, 13). It is this question of what it means to be human that hovers over Iago, that 'inhuman dog' as Roderigo calls him in his dying line (5.1.62). Shakespeare's presentation of Iago follows on from Marlowe's *Jew of Malta* where Marlowe poses the question: what does evil look like

in a (political) world where devils no longer have forked tails
and cloven feet, in a (theatrical) world where devils are no
longer accompanied by fireworks? How do we recognize the
devil when we see him? It is easy to characterize the Other as
monstrous – the prosthetic nose of Marlowe's Barabas or the
skin colour of Othello – and to embroider the stereotype. But
in fact the real monster may no longer be so easily or stereo-
typically identified. He looks like us.

Questions about the monstrous can be linked to the play's
investigation of women; Carol Rutter suggests that the play's
true monsters are husbands (Rutter, 166). They are the
cannibals, the 'household anthropophagi' who, as Emilia says,
'eat us hungrily, and when they are full, / They belch us' (3.4
104–7).

Epistemology

The topic of monsters, like all of the topics above, is part of
a larger single investigation in the play: of epistemology (the
science of knowing). How do we know anything?

The play's polarized subjects and images – of stereotyped
black behaviour, of idealized women's behaviour, of characters'
alleged motivations, of the natural and unnatural – are all part
of this central investigation. How do we decide between Iago's
competing motivations? How do we decide which of the
play's women is a whore? How do we decide which is the true
narrative of the handkerchief? In short: how do we interpret
evidence? (Language is relevant here, as we saw in Chapter
1 where the play's parallel linguistic structures and imprecise
grammatical referents make it different to tell which is the
'right' reading.) Narrative comes into this investigation too.
Iago is a slanderer; Othello a story-teller. The two are linked:
'Both the slanderer and the story-teller give to their hearers a
new world, a new mind (along with a new language)' (Gross,
841). Both conjure up fictions but Iago's is a brazen world,

Othello's a golden. Or, to put it more accurately, Othello makes worlds but Iago *un*makes them. His capacity is not for creation but for destruction.

Because of its interest in how language makes and unmakes worlds, the play encourages us to be on our guard: in ascribing causes, interpreting evidence, drawing conclusions, assigning motives, making judgements. There can be no better advice for approaching this text (and all texts), for assembling and analysing evidence, and for writing an essay. *Othello* is its own writing manual: the play cautions against hasty conclusions and unexamined assumptions, and makes a plea for us to be hyper-sensitive to the implications of the language we hear, read and write.

BIBLIOGRAPHY
AND FURTHER
READING

Adamson, Sylvia, Lynette Hunter, Lynne Magnusson, Ann
    Thompson and Katie Wales, *Reading Shakespeare's Dramatic
    Language: A Guide* (London: Arden Shakespeare, 2001).
Altman, Joel, *The Improbability of Othello* (Chicago: University of
    Chicago Press, 2010).
Anouilh, Jean, *Antigone* in *Plays: I*, intro. Ned Chaillet (London:
    Methuen, 1987).
Augustine of Hippo, Bishop, *The Teacher (De Magistro)* in *Against
    the Academicians: The Teacher*, trans. Peter King (Indianapolis:
    Hackett, 1995).
Bartels, Emily C., *Speaking of the Moor: From Alcazar to Othello*
    (Philadelphia, PA: University of Pennsylvania Press, 2008).
Barton, Anne, *Ben Jonson, Dramatist* (Cambridge: Cambridge
    University Press, 1984).
Bate, Jonathan, *The Romantics on Shakespeare* (Harmondsworth:
    Penguin, 1992).
—'The Bawdy Court', in Paul Raffield and Gary Watt (eds),
    Shakespeare and the Law (Oxford: Hart, 2008), 41–50.
Beale, Simon Russell, Lecture to the British Psychoanalytic Society.
    Reprinted in National Theatre programme for *Timon of Athens*,
    2012.
Berry, Philippa, 'Hamlet's Ear', *Shakespeare Survey* 50 (1997), 57–64.
Berry, Philippa and Margaret Tudeau-Clayton, *Textures of
    Renaissance Knowledge* (Manchester: Manchester University
    Press, 2004).
Bhabha, Homi, *The Location of Culture* (London: Routledge,
    1994).
Bible (Geneva, 1560; London, 1576).

Boose, Lynda E., 'The Recognizance and Pledge of Love', *English Literary Renaissance* 5 (1975), 360–74.

Bradshaw, Graham, 'Othello in the Age of Cognitive Science', *Shakespeare Studies* (Tokyo, Japan), 38 (2000), 17–38.

—*The Connell Guide to Shakespeare's Othello* (London: Connell Guides, 2010).

Brantley, Ben, 'A Down-to-Earth Iago, Evil Made Ordinary', *New York Times*, 11 April 1998 http://www.nytimes.com/1998/04/11/theater/theater-review-a-down-to-earth-iago-evil-made-ordinary.html

Brockbank, J. P., *On Shakespeare: Jesus, Shakespeare and Karl Marx and Other Essays* (Oxford: Basil Blackwell, 1989).

Bruster, Douglas, 'Teaching *Othello* as Tragedy and Comedy', in Erickson and Hunt, 100–7.

Burckhardt, Sigurd, *The Drama of Language* (Baltimore, MD: Johns Hopkins University Press, 1970).

Byron, *Don Juan* in *The Major Works*, ed. Jerome McGann (Oxford: Oxford University Press, 2008).

Calderwood, James L., 'Speech and Self in *Othello*', *Shakespeare Quarterly* 38 (1987), 293–303.

Callaghan, Dympna, '"Othello was a white man": Properties of Race on Shakespeare's Stage' in *Shakespeare without Women* (London: Routledge, 2000), 75–96.

Cannon, Christopher, 'Proverbs and the Wisdom of Literature: The Proverbs of Alfred and Chaucer's Tale of Melibee', *Textual Practice* 24:3 (2010), 407–34.

Chambers, E. K., *The Elizabethan Stage*, vols 2 and 4 (Oxford: Clarendon Press, 1923).

Chakrabarti, Lolita, *Red Velvet* (London: Methuen Drama, 2012).

Coghill, Nevill, *Shakespeare's Professional Skills* (Cambridge: Cambridge University Press, 1964).

Coleridge, Samuel Taylor, *Lectures 1808–1819: On Literature,* ed. R. A. Foakes, 2 vols (London: Routledge and Kegan Paul; Princeton, NJ: Princeton University Press, 1987).

—*Shorter Works and Fragments*, ed. H. J. Jackson and J. R. de J. Jackson, 2 vols (London: Routledge; Princeton, NJ: Princeton University Press, 1995).

Colet, John and William Lily, *A Shorte Introduction of Grammar* (1567), introduced by Vincent J. Flynn (Delmar, NY: Scholars' Facsimiles, 1977).

Corbett, Edward P. J. and P. J. Connors, *Classical Rhetoric for the Modern Student* (New York: Oxford University Press, 1998).

Craig, Hugh, 'Grammatical Modality in English Plays from the 1580s to the 1640s', *English Literary Renaissance* 30:1 (2000), 32–54.

Culler, Jonathan (ed.), *On Puns: The Foundation of Letters* (Oxford: Blackwell, 1988).

Daileader, Celia, *Racism, Misogyny and the 'Othello' Myth* (Cambridge: Cambridge University Press, 2005).

De Grazia, Margreta, '"Lost Potential in Grammar and Nature": Sidney's *Astrophil and Stella*', *Studies in English Literature 1500–1900* 21 (1981), 21–35.

Dorval, Patricia, 'Shakespeare on Screen: Threshold Aesthetics in Oliver Parker's *Othello*', *Early Modern Literary Studies* 6:1 (May 2000): 1.1–15, URL: http://purl.oclc.org/emls/06-1/dorvothe.htm.

Dundas, Judith, '*Paronomasia* in the Quip Modest: From Sidney to Herbert', *Connotations* 2:3 (1992), 223–33.

Eggins, Suzanne and Diane Slade, *Analysing Casual Conversation* (London: Cassell 1997).

Eliot, T. S., *Selected Essays* (London: Faber and Faber, 1951).

Enterline, Lynn, *The Rhetoric of the Body from Ovid to Shakespeare* (Cambridge: Cambridge University Press, 2000).

Erickson, Peter and Maurice Hunt (eds), *Approaches to Teaching 'Othello'* (New York: Modern Languages Association, 2005).

Fine, Gail, 'Plato on Naming', *Philosophical Quarterly* 27 (1977), 289–301.

Ford, John, *Love's Sacrifice*, ed. A. T. Moore. Revels edition (Manchester, Manchester University Press, 2002).

Fowler, Alastair, *Kinds of Literature: An Introduction to the Theory of Genres and Methods* (Oxford: Clarendon Press, 1982, reprinted 2002).

Garnier-Giamarchi, Marie, 'Mobility and the Method: From Shakespeare's Treatise on Mab to Descartes' *Treatise on Man*', in Philippa Berry and Margaret Tudeau-Clayton (eds), *Textures of Renaissance Knowledge* (Manchester: Manchester University Press, 2004), 137–55.

Greenblatt, Stephen, *Renaissance Self-Fashioning* (Chicago: University of Chicago Press, 1980).

Grennan, Eamon, 'Arm and Sleeve: Nature and Custom in *Comedy of Errors*', *Philological Quarterly* 59 (1980), 150–64.

Gross, Kenneth, 'Slender and Skepticism in *Othello*', *English Literary History* 56: 4 (1989), 819–52.

Hadfield, Andrew, *Literature, Travel and Colonial Writing in the English Renaissance 1545–1625* (Oxford: Oxford University Press, 2007).

Hall, Kim F., *Things of Darkness: Economies of Race and Gender in Early Modern England* (Ithaca, NY, Cornell University Press, 1995).

Hankey, Julie (ed.), *Othello (Shakespeare in Production)*, 2nd edn (Cambridge: Cambridge University Press, 2005).

Harris, Amanda, 'Emilia', in Michael Dobson (ed.), *Performing Shakespeare's Tragedies Today* (Cambridge: Cambridge University Press, 2006), pp. 71–82.

Harris, Roy and Talbot J. Taylor, *Landmarks in Linguistic Thought* (London: Routledge, 1989).

Hartman, Geoffrey, *Beyond Formalism: Literary Essays 1958–70* (New Haven, CT: Yale University Press, 1970).

Hawthorn, Jeremy, *Unlocking the Text: Fundamental Issues in Literary Theory* (London: Edward Arnold, 1987).

Heywood, Thomas, *The Fair Maid of the Exchange with Fortune by Land and Sea* (by Thomas Heywood and Samuel Rowley), ed. Barron Field (London: The Shakespeare Society, 1846).

Holderness, Graham, Nick Potter and John Turner, *Shakespeare: The Play of History* (Iowa City: University of Iowa Press, 1988).

Holland, Peter, 'The Resources of Characterization in *Othello*', *Shakespeare Survey* 41 (1989), 119–32.

Honigmann, E. A. J., *The Stability of Shakespeare's Text* (London: Edward Arnold, 1965).

—*The Texts of 'Othello' and Shakespearian Revision* (London: Routledge, 1996).

Hope, Jonathan, *Shakespeare Language: Reason, Eloquence and Artifice in the Renaissance*. Arden Shakespeare Library (London: Methuen, 2010).

— and Michael Witmore, 'The Hundredth Psalm to the Tune of "Green Sleeves": Digital Approaches to Shakespeare's Language of Genre', *Shakespeare Quarterly* 61:3 (2010), 357–390.

Hopkins, Lisa, '"And shall I die, and this unconquered?": Marlowe's Inverted Colonialism', *Early Modern Literary Studies* 2.2 (1996), 1.1–23, URL: http://purl.oclc.org/emls/02-2/hopkmarl.html

—'Review of *Othello*. Adapted for Television by Andrew Davies', *Early Modern Literary Studies* 8.1 (2002), 11.1–4, URL: http://purl.oclc.org/emls/08-1/othellorev.htm

Howard, Jean E., 'An English Lass Amid the Moors: Gender, Race, Sexuality, and National Identity in Heywood's *The Fair Maid of the West*' in Margo Hendricks and Patricia Parker (eds), *Women, 'Race' and Writing in the Early Modern Period* (London: Routledge, 1994), 101–17.

—'*Othello* as an Adventure Play' in Erickson and Hunt, 90–9.

Hunter, G. K., *Othello and Colour Prejudice* (Oxford: Oxford University Press, 1967).

Hutson, Lorna, 'Forensic Aspects of Renaissance Mimesis', *Representations* 94 (2006), 80–109.

Ingelby, C. M., *Shakespeare the Man and the Book, Part Two* (*Papers on Shakespeare*) (London: Trübner, 1881).

Iser, Wolfgang, *How To Do Theory* (Oxford: Blackwell, 2006).

Jardine, Lisa, *Reading Shakespeare Historically* (London: Routledge, 1996).

Jauss, Hans, *Towards an Aesthetic of Reception* (Brighton: Harvester, 1982).

Jones, Eldred, *Othello's Countrymen: The African in English Renaissance Drama* (London: Oxford University Press, 1965).

Jones, Emrys, *Scenic Form in Shakespeare* (Oxford: Clarendon Press, 1971).

Jonson, Ben, *Ben Jonson: Works*, C. H. Hereford and Percy and Evelyn Simpson (eds), 11 vols (Oxford: Clarendon Press, 1925–52), vol. 8.

—*Every Man in his Humour*, ed. Robert S. Miola, Revels edition (Manchester: Manchester University Press, 2000).

—*Poetaster* in *The Devil is an Ass and Other Plays*, ed. M. J. Kidnie (Oxford: Oxford University Press, 2000).

Kermode, Frank, *Shakespeare's Language* (London: Penguin, 2000).

Knight, G. Wilson, *The Wheel of Fire: Interpretations of Shakespearean Tragedy* (New York: Meridian, 1957).

Kolentsis, Alysia, '"Mark You / His Absolute Shall?": Multitudinous Tongues and Contested Words in *Coriolanus*', *Shakespeare Survey* 62 (2009), 141–50.

Leggatt, Alexander, *Shakespeare's Tragedies: Violation and Identity* (Cambridge: Cambridge University Press, 2005).

—'Teen Shakespeare: *10 Things I Hate About You* and *O*', in Paul

Nelson and June Schlueter (eds), *Acts of Criticism: Performance Matters in Shakespeare and his Contemporaries* (Cranbury, NJ: Associated University Presses, 2006), 245–58.

Lucking, David, 'Putting Out the Light: Semantic Indeterminacy and the Deconstitution of Self in *Othello*', *English Studies* 75 (1994), 110–22.

Magnusson, Lynne, 'A Play of Modals: Grammar and Potential Action in Early Shakespeare', *Shakespeare Survey* 62 (2009), 69–80.

Maguire, Laurie and Emma Smith, '"Time's Comic Sparks": *The Dramaturgy of A Mad World, My Masters* and *Timon of Athens*' in Gary Taylor and Trish Thomas Henley (eds), *The Oxford Handbook of Thomas Middleton* (Oxford: Oxford University Press, 2012), 181–95.

Mamet, David, *Oleanna* (London: Vintage Books, 2002).

Manningham, John, *Diary of John Manningham*, ed. John Bruce (London: 1886).

Marlowe, Christopher, *Complete Plays and Poems*, E. D. Pendry and J. C. Maxwell (eds) (London: J. M. Dent, 1976).

—*Dr Faustus, A- and B-texts*, David Bevington and Eric Rasmussen (eds), Revels series (Manchester: Manchester University Press, 1993).

McBain, James, *Early Tudor Drama and Legal Culture* (unpublished D.Phil. thesis, University of Oxford, 2007).

McCabe, Richard, 'Iago in *Othello*', in Robert Smallwood (ed.), *Players of Shakespeare 5* (Cambridge: Cambridge University Press, 2003), 192–211.

McDonald, Russ, *Shakespeare and the Arts of Language* (Oxford: Oxford University Press, 2000).

Melchiori, Giorgio, 'The Rhetoric of Character Construction: *Othello*', *Shakespeare Survey* 34 (1981), 61–72.

Michael, Ian, *English Grammatical Categories and the Tradition to 1800* (Cambridge: Cambridge University Press, 1970).

Mooney, Michael E., 'Location and Idiom in *Othello*' in Virginia Vaughan and Kent Cartwright (eds), *Othello: New Perspectives* (London and Toronto: Associated University Presses, 1991), 115–34.

Morgan, Ben, *Absent Presences: Four Paratheatrical Characters in Shakespeare's Plays* (unpublished D. Phil thesis, University of Oxford, 2008).

Neill, Michael, 'Changing Places in *Othello*', *Shakespeare Survey* 37
    (1984), 115–31.
—'"Mulattos", "Blacks", and "Indian Moors": *Othello* and Early
    Modern Constructions of Human Difference', *Shakespeare
    Quarterly* 49 (1998), 361–74.
—'"His Master's Ass": Slavery, Service and Subordination in
    Othello', in Thomas Clayton, Susan Brock and Vincent Forés
    (eds), Shakespeare and the Mediterranean (Newark, DE:
    University of Delaware Press, 2004a) 215–29.
—'"Servile ministers": Othello, King Lear and the Sacralization of
    Service', in Brian Boyd (ed.), *Words that Count* (Newark, DE:
    University of Delaware Press, 2004b), 161–80.
—'*Othello* and Race' in Erickson and Hunt, 37–52.
Nuttall, A. D., *Shakespeare the Thinker* (Oxford: Oxford University
    Press, 2007).
Palfrey, Simon, *Doing Shakespeare*, second edition (London: Arden
    Shakespeare, 2011).
— and Tiffany Stern, *Shakespeare in Parts* (Oxford: Oxford
    University Press, 2007).
Parker, Patricia, 'Shakespeare and Rhetoric: "Dilation" and
    "Delation" in *Othello*', in Patricia Parker and Geoffrey Hartman
    (eds), *Shakespeare and the Question of Theory* (London:
    Methuen, 1985), 54–74.
Peacham, Henry, *The Garden of Eloquence (1593)* (Gainesville, FL:
    Scholars' Facsimiles and Reprints, 1954).
Pechter, Edward, *'Othello' and Interpretive Traditions* (Iowa City,
    IO: University of Iowa Press, 1999), p.188.
Potter, Lois, *The Life of William Shakespeare: A Critical Biography*
    (Oxford: Wiley-Blackwell, 2012).
—*Othello: Shakespeare in Performance* (Manchester: Manchester
    University Press, 2002).
Pryse, Marjorie, 'Lust for Audience: An Interpretation of *Othello*',
    English Literary History 43 (1976), 461–78.
Puttenham, George, *The Arte of English Poesie*, Gladys Willcock
    and Alice Walker (eds) (Cambridge: Cambridge University Press,
    1936).
Quarshie, Hugh, *Second Thoughts about 'Othello'*, International
    Shakespeare Association Occasional Papers 7 (Chipping
    Campden, UK, International Shakespeare Association, 1999).
Redfern, Walter, *Puns* (Oxford: Blackwell, 1984).

Rosenthal, Daniel, 'Inspector Moor', *The Observer*, 25 November 2001, *Review* section, 7.

Rissanen, Matti, 'Syntax' in *The Cambridge History of the English Language*, 6 vols (Cambridge: Cambridge University Press, 1999), vol. 3, 187–330.

Rutter, Carol Chillington, *Enter the Body* (London: Routledge, 2001).

Rymer, Thomas, *A Short View of Tragedy*, ed. Curt Zimansky, *The Critical Works of Thomas Rymer* (New Haven: Yale University Press, 1956), 132–64.

Serpieri, Alessandro, 'Reading the Signs: Towards a Semiotics of Shakespearean Drama', trans. by Keir Elam in John Drakakis (ed.), *Alternative Shakespeares* (London: Methuen, 1985), 119–43.

Shakespeare, William, *The Riverside Shakespeare*, G. B. Evans (gen. ed.) (Boston: Houghton Mifflin, 1974).

—*The Comedy of Errors*, ed. R. A. Foakes (London: Arden Shakespeare, 1968).

—*Coriolanus*, ed. Philip Brockbank (London: Arden Shakespeare, 1976).

—*Hamlet*, ed. Harold Jenkins (London: Arden Shakespeare, 1982).

—*Julius Caesar*, ed. David Daniell (London: Arden Shakespeare, 1998).

—*King Henry IV, Part 1*, ed. David Scott Kastan (London: Arden Shakespeare, 2003).

—*King Henry V*, ed. T. W. Craik (London: Arden Shakespeare, 1995).

—*King Lear*, ed. R. A. Foakes (London: Arden Shakespeare, 1997).

—*King Richard II*, ed. Charles R. Forker (London: Arden Shakespeare, 2002).

—*King Richard III*, ed. Antony Hammond (London: Arden Shakespeare, 1982).

—*Macbeth*, ed. Kenneth Muir (London: Arden Shakespeare, 1997).

—*Measure for Measure*, ed. J. W. Lever (London: Arden Shakespeare, 1968).

—*Much Ado About Nothing*, ed. A. R. Humphreys (London: Arden Shakespeare, 1982).

—*Othello*, ed. E. A. J. Honigmann (London: Arden Shakespeare, 1997, reprinted 2001).

—*Othello*, ed. Michael Neill (Oxford: Oxford University Press, 2006).

—*The First Quarto of Othello*, ed. Scott McMillin (Cambridge: Cambridge University Press, 2005).

—*Pericles*, ed. Suzanne Gossett (London: Arden Shakespeare: 2004).

—*Romeo and Juliet*, ed. Brian Gibbons (London: Arden Shakespeare, 1980).

—*The Taming of the Shrew*, ed. Brian Morris (London: Arden Shakespeare, 1982).

—*The Taming of the Shrew*, ed. Barbara Hodgdon (London: Arden, 2010).

—*Timon of Athens*, ed. H. J. Oliver (London: Arden Shakespeare, 1969).

—*Timon of Athens*, Anthony B. Dawson and Gretchen E. Minton (eds) (London: Arden Shakespeare, 2008).

—*Troilus and Cressida*, ed. David Bevington (London: Arden Shakespeare, 1998).

—*Twelfth Night*, ed. Keir Elam (London: Arden Shakespeare, 2008).

—*The Two Gentlemen of Verona*, ed. William C. Carroll (London: Arden Shakespeare, 2004).

—*The Winter's Tale*, ed. J. H. Pafford (London: Arden Shakespeare, 1966).

—*The Winter's Tale*, ed. John Pitcher (London: Arden Shakespeare, 2010).

—*The Winter's Tale*, ed. Stephen Orgel (Oxford: Oxford University Press, 1996).

Shaw, Jonathan, programme article, *Othello*, National Theatre 2013. Also printed as 'Othello's Military Significance', *Evening Standard*, 23 April 2013 and available online: http://www.standard.co.uk/goingout/theatre/exarmy-officer-jonathan-shaw-on-othellos-military-significance-8583965.html (accessed 10 September 2013).

Sher, Sir Antony, 'Iago', in Michael Dobson (ed.), *Performing Shakespeare's Tragedies Today* (Cambridge: Cambridge University Press, 2006), 56–69.

Sidney, Sir Philip, *The Old Arcadia,* ed. Katherine Duncan-Jones (Oxford: Oxford University Press, 1985).

—*Sir Philip Sidney*, ed. Katherine Duncan-Jones (Oxford: Oxford University Press, 1989).

Smallwood, R. L. "'*Tis Pity She's a Whore* and *Romeo and Juliet*', *Cahiers Elisabéthains* 20 (1981), 49–70.

Smith, Emma, *Othello* (Devon: Northcote House, 2005).

—*Macbeth* (Bloomsbury: London, 2013).

Smith, Ian, 'Othello's Black Handkerchief', *Shakespeare Quarterly* 64:1 (2013), 1–25.

Snyder, Susan, *The Comic Matrix of Shakespeare's Tragedies* (Princeton: Princeton University Press, 1979).

—'The Genres of Shakespeare's Plays', in Margreta de Grazia and Stanley Wells (eds), *The Cambridge Companion to Shakespeare* (Cambridge: Cambridge University Press, 2001), 83–98.

Stallybrass, Peter, 'Patriarchal Territories: The Body Enclosed', in Margaret W. Ferguson, Maureen Quilligan and Nancy J. Vickers (eds), *Rewriting the Renaissance: The Discourses of Sexual Difference in Early Modern Europe* (Chicago: University of Chicago Press, 1986), 123–42.

States, Bert O., *Great Reckonings in Little Rooms: On the Phenomenology of Theater* (Los Angeles, CA: University of California Press, 1987).

Stoppard, Tom, *Rosencrantz and Guildenstern are Dead* (London: Faber and Faber, 1973).

Suchet, David, 'Iago in *Othello*' in Russell Jackson and Robert Smallwood (eds), *Players of Shakespeare,* vol. 2 (Cambridge: Cambridge University Press, 1998), 179–99.

Tanner, Tony, *Adultery and the Novel* (Baltimore, MD: Johns Hopkins University Press, 1979, reprinted 1981).

—*Prefaces to Shakespeare* (Cambridge, MA: Harvard University Press, 2010).

Terentius Publius Afer, *Terence, with an English translation by John Sargeaunt*, Loeb Classical Library, 2 vols (London: William Heinemann, 1912).

Toole, James, '"I good remedy therfore may & will speake ..." "Remedy" and "No Remedy" in the Renaissance' (unpublished paper).

Toye, Richard, *Rhetoric: A very Short Introduction* (Oxford: Oxford University Press, 2013).

Tyson, Rikita, 'What they will: comic grammar in *Twelfth Night*' (forthcoming in *Shakespeare*) http://www.tandfonline.com/doi/abs/10.1080/17450918.2013.766252

Ulmer, Gregory, 'The Puncept in Grammatology' in *On Puns: The Foundation of Letters*, ed. Jonathan Culler (Oxford: Blackwell, 1988), 164–90.

Watson, Robert N., 'Tragedy' in A. R. Braunmuller and Michael Hattaway (eds), *The Cambridge Companion to English Renaissance Tragedy* (Cambridge: Cambridge University Press, 1990), 301–51.

Wayne, Valerie, 'The Sexual Politics of Textual Transmission' in Laurie E. Maguire and Thomas L. Berger (eds), *Textual Formations and Reformations* (Newark, DE: University of Delaware Press, 1998), 179–210.

Wilder, Lisa Perkins, *Shakespeare's Memory Theatre* (Cambridge: Cambridge University Press, 2010).

Williams, Wes, *Monsters and their Meanings in Early Modern Culture: Mighty Magic* (Oxford: Oxford University Press, 2011).

Wilson, Edwin, *Shaw on Shakespeare* (London: Applause Theatre Books, 2002).

Wright, George T. 'Hendiadys and Hamlet', *PMLA* 96:2 (1981), 168–193.

Yachnin, Paul, 'Wonder-Effects: Othello's Handkerchief' in Jonathan Gil Harris and Natasha Korda (eds), *Staged Properties in Early Modern English Drama* (Cambridge: Cambridge University Press, 2006).

Filmography

Othello directed by Orson Welles (1952).
Othello directed by Stuart Burge (1965).
Othello directed by Jonathan Miller (1981).
Othello directed by Trevor Nunn (1989).
Othello directed by Oliver Parker (1995).
Othello directed by Janet Suzman (2005).
Othello directed by Wilson Milam (2007).
Verdi, *Otello* directed by Franco Zeffirelli (1986).

Adaptations

O directed by Tim Blake Nelson (2001).
Othello directed by Geoffrey Sax (2001).
Stage Beauty directed by Richard Eyre (2004).